SURVEY THE SCRIPTURES

BASIC BIBLE COMMENTARY

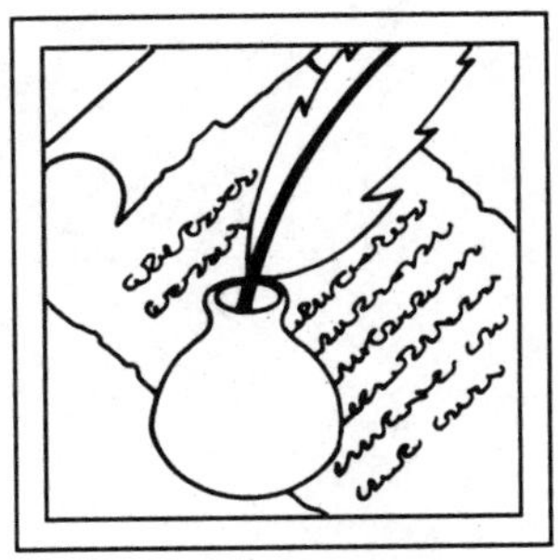

# Romans

## Amazing Grace

Dr. Edgar C. James

MERIDIAN®

This edition is published by special arrangement with and permission of Moody External Studies. Revised edition by Moody External Studies of the USA.



Note: Archaic expressions, spellings, and punctuation have been updated in some Bible verses.

M20 Paperback Study Edition
ISBN: 0-529-06950-4

Cover design by Gayle Raymer
Book Design by Blue Water Ink

A Meridian Publication
Published with World Bible Publishers

Printed in the United States of America

# Contents

# *Preface*

To begin to understand the specifics of in-depth Bible study, we must have a grasp of how the entire Bible fits together and the basic theme of each Bible book.

*Survey of the Scriptures* first takes us on an exciting tour through the Bible, relating one section to another. So that by knowing how each part relates to the others we can better appreciate and apply its lessons for us.

Since June 1973 Dr. Edgar James has taught New Testament studies at Moody Bible Institute, including this basic Bible study guide. For almost fifteen years the summary of his work has been published as a Bible correspondence course for the External Studies division of Moody Bible Institute.

Now for the first time, this incisive and insightful commentary is available for personal or group Bible study to help readers see the Scriptures as an interrelated unit with a plan, a plot, and a purpose, and to provide a more in-depth look at each individual book of the Bible.

—The Publisher

# Introduction

To see the Bible as a whole is not only vital to a proper understanding of the Bible; it can also be a thrilling experience!

This book and others in the Survey of the Scripture series provide study material on individual books of the Bible for a closer look at specific areas of Scripture.

Today, as always, people must be brought face to face with the fact that sin is personal and separates them from God. We need a renewed appreciation of God's righteousness at a time when many have an increasingly tolerant attitude toward sin; we need an understanding of the concept of justification by faith at a time when people are boasting in their good works. These themes are found in the book of Romans.

This commentary, rather than being a complete study of the book of Romans, attempts to furnish an introduction to start you on a lifetime of Bible study and Christian growth.

Because these materials were initially used both as classroom and correspondence school texts, the style is one of a teacher—guiding, challenging, directing, stimulating, and raising questions as well as providing answers.

The author, Dr. Edgar C. James, is professor of theology at Moody Bible Institute. Dr. James explains the complex content of the book of Romans clearly and warmly, emphasizing the joy to be found by living a life in keeping with God's righteousness through Christ.

The content of this edition is taken from an adult credit course from Moody Bible Institute, External Studies Division. For information on how you might take this and other courses for credit, write for a free catalog to:

Moody External Studies
Moody Bible Institute
820 N. La Salle
Chicago, IL 60610

# 1

# An Overview

"I might have a prosperous journey by the will of God to come unto you" (Romans 1:10).

---

Have you ever asked yourself, "What really is the Bible all about?" Perhaps you have begun reading at the beginning of the Old or New Testament and have gotten bogged down. "If there were only some key book," you tell yourself, "one that would explain sin and salvation, the Christian life and how to live it, the reasons for the believer's faith, life, and hope. I would not only read such a book, but I would do what it says."

Some time ago a group of people had a similar point of view. They needed to know what the Christian life was all about. They needed to be established in the fundamentals of the faith. These people were believers living in the city of Rome. The apostle Paul wrote a letter to them that expounds the truths of the Gospel they had already accepted.

Every book of the Bible is profitable for believers to study. But the book of Romans, which has been called "the constitution of Christianity," is crucial because it carefully explains the doctrines most necessary for a correct understanding of the Christian faith. It treats matters of interest to believers throughout the centuries. Are the heathen lost? How can a condemned sinner stand in the presence of a holy God? Is it actually possible to live a Christian life?

The Swiss commentator Godet pointed out that every revival movement in the history of the Christian church has been connected with the teachings found in Romans.

## THE PLACE OF ROMANS IN THE BIBLE

Viewed from our point in history, the New Testament may be divided into three major sections: a past, a present, and a future. The Gospels and Acts form the historical foundation on which our faith is built. The four Gospels narrate the life of Christ, with each Gospel stressing a different aspect of his ministry. Together they present a fourfold picture of his life, death, and resurrection. The book of Acts gives the history of the founding, establishment, and outreach of the early church.

The Epistles explain the historical events recorded in the Gospels and Acts. They declare the meaning of the life and death of Jesus Christ and give reasons for the resurrection. They define the nature, make-up, and mission of the church that was founded on the day of Pentecost. They instruct members of the church in matters pertaining to life and witness, abilities and responsibilities. The Epistles give standards and instructions for believers today.

The book of Revelation is the consummating book of the New Testament and of the entire Bible. It presents that which is yet future. So we see that the Christian faith is grounded on historical fact, has carefully explained doctrines, and gives an outline of future events.

Of the twenty-one books that comprise the Epistles of the New Testament, the apostle Paul wrote at least thirteen and possibly fourteen (Hebrews being the fourteenth). Of these books, Romans, Corinthians, and Ephesians were written to particular churches. Timothy, Titus, and Philemon were written to individuals. Paul also wrote: Galatians, Philippians, Colossians, and 1 and 2 Thessalonians.

The nature of the Epistles is different from that of the Gospels and Acts. The Epistles all refer to the salvation Christ accomplished at Calvary as the basis for what they teach. They are addressed to believers as a group, not to Jews or Gentiles as such. And they are all in letter form, which makes them interesting and personal.

Although the book of Romans stands first in the order of the Epistles, it was not written first. Of Paul's writings, 1 Thessalonians was probably written first, and 2 Timothy last. However, neither of these is at the beginning or ending of the order we have in our Bibles.

Romans stands first in the order of the Epistles because of its length (it is the longest epistle) and also because of its importance. It explains the doctrines of sin and salvation, the meaning of the cross, the reasons for the believer's faith, life, and hope. It is a gateway connecting the other Epistles to the Gospels and Acts.

Great men throughout the centuries have testified that this book has had great effect on their lives. An early church father, Chrysostom, had the entire epistle read to him twice a week. The reformer Melanchthon copied it twice by hand in order to know it better. Martin Luther's life was changed by the verse "The just shall live by faith" (Romans 1:17), and his life in turn changed the course of history. Of this book he said, "The epistle to the Romans is the true masterpiece of the New Testament and the very purest gospel, which is well worth and deserving that a Christian man should not only learn it by heart, word for word, but also that he should daily deal with it as the daily bread of men's souls. It can never be too much or too well read or studied, and the more it is handled the more precious it becomes, and the better it tastes."

## THE WRITER OF THE BOOK

The intellectual world of the apostle Paul's day was searching for truth, much like our world today. Jewish philosophy that had held sway for some time was in rampant decay. The Greeks and Romans had carried their polytheism to such an extreme that it began to defy imagination. The climate was one of complete skepticism, but also one of hunger for the Gospel.

Into this world the Lord placed a man he had prepared to know and declare his message. Paul was born in the Greek city of Tarsus, the capital of Cilicia. Tarsus was northwest of Palestine in what today is modern Turkey. It was an academic center on a level with Alexandria and Athens. As a result of his fine education, Paul thought carefully and logically. He had mastered the Greek language, the common language of his world. Furthermore, he was a Roman citizen. This gave him many advantages because the world was dominated by the Roman Empire.

And Paul was also a Jew. He was educated in the ways of Judaism by his parents and later in the school of Gamaliel in Jerusalem. He knew and loved the Old Testament, and he also knew and loved the Jewish people. Although he was the minister to the Gentiles, his heart's desire was that Israel might be saved (Romans 10:1).

Earlier in his life, when still an adherent of Judaism, Paul had tried to stamp out the Christian faith, which he considered a heresy. He was on the way to Damascus to destroy the church when he was converted. After that, he spent three years in Arabia and then returned to Damascus. But there he was persecuted for his faith and eventually had to flee for his life. He then went to Jerusalem and from there to Tarsus, which is where he was when Barnabas called him to come and help with the work at Antioch. This church sent him on three missionary journeys whereby he established other churches and instructed the believers through his writings. Later he was arrested in Jerusalem, imprisoned in Caesarea, and finally sent to Rome. He was imprisoned there twice. He died in A.D. 66.

## THE CHURCH AT ROME

Paul wrote most of his epistles to churches he had established and visited. But he had not visited the church in Rome when he wrote to it. Colossians is the only other epistle Paul wrote to a church he did not visit.

Who founded the church at Rome? There is no historical evidence for the theory that Peter founded this church, and a great deal of evidence against it. There is no mention of Peter in Romans. It is doubtful that Romans would have been written at all if Peter had been there. Paul had said emphatically that he did not want to build on another man's foundation (Romans 15:20).

It is also doubtful that this church was founded by Jewish converts from Rome who were in Jerusalem on the day of Pentecost. An examination of the names given in Romans 16 shows that the church at Rome consisted mostly of Gentiles, not Jews. Moreover, Paul was regarded as the spiritual leader of this church when he finally arrived there (Acts 28). The fact that Paul, rather than Peter, wrote Romans also shows his authority there.

The most probable theory is that converts of Paul's ministry on his missionary journeys came to Rome for business reasons and founded the church there. At that time the Roman Empire was at its zenith, and the city of Rome was the center of the earth.

Rome was founded in 753 B.C. and was named after its founder Romulus. It was located along the Tiber River about seventeen miles from the Mediterranean Sea. During the time of the early church, a network of roads went from Rome to all parts of the empire. Many people traveled to the city. Every Roman citizen hoped to eventually visit this place of central authority. The apostle had evidently heard of the believers there through Aquila and Priscilla, as well as from others he had met on his travels.

The apostle probably was considered this church's spiritual father because he had indirectly founded it. This would also explain why so many Gentiles are mentioned in his personal greetings (Romans 16). But most of all, this gives insight as to why he took so much time to carefully instruct these people whom he had never seen.

Although the church at Rome was predominantly Gentile, there was a large Jewish population within the city, which dated from 63 B.C., when the Roman General Pompey captured Jerusalem. Many Jews were brought to Rome and sold as slaves. However, because of their religious conflict with Roman polytheism, they did not fit into the Roman social structure and were released from slavery. The Romans were lenient toward them and allowed them to have their own synagogue and to found a colony on the farther side of the Tiber. This colony soon became a part of the city itself.

The church in Rome was a mixture of believers from the lower classes, who had been slaves, and many from the upper classes as well, even some of Caesar's household. The church was loosely organized. One of the meeting places was the house of Aquila and Priscilla (Romans 16:5).

## THE OCCASION AND DATE

Paul wrote this letter because of his burning desire to visit this church. He wanted to prepare the believers for his visit and to give them sound instruction in the faith. Moreover, Phoebe was in Corinth when Paul wrote the letter and was going to make a trip to Rome. This provided Paul the opportunity to send a letter with her.

A careful study of Romans shows when the book was written. An offering had been given by the Greek churches for the needy believers in Jerusalem. Paul wanted to take it to them (Romans 15:25–26). In the book of Acts, we find that on the third missionary journey, Paul left Ephesus, visited the churches in Achaia (Greece), and then proceeded to Jerusalem in A.D. 58. Therefore, it is possible to ascertain that he wrote the book of Romans in A.D. 58.

That Paul wrote the book in Corinth is established from the names in chapter 16. Phoebe, who carried the letter to Rome, was an active participant in the church of Cenchreae, the harbor of Corinth. Gaius, mentioned in Romans 16:23, was an early convert in Corinth (1 Corinthians 1:14), and Erastus, the treasurer of the city (Romans 16:23), was also from Corinth (2 Timothy 4:20).

## THE THEME OF THE BOOK

The theme of the book of Romans is given in the first chapter. Paul writes, "For I am not ashamed of the gospel of Christ . . . for therein is the righteousness of God revealed from faith to faith: as it is written, The just shall live by faith" (Romans 1:16–17).

The theme of the book of Romans is *righteousness*, particularly the righteousness of God, which he gives to those who believe in him, whereby he can declare them perfect in his sight. Our own human righteousness is "as filthy rags" (Isaiah 64:6). So if we are to be rightly related to God, we must have some righteousness other than our own. This righteousness can only come from God. The book of Romans explains the details involved in the transmission of God's righteousness to us—God reveals it and we receive it.

First, Romans presents the *revelation* of God's righteousness. This righteousness is revealed in the Gospel. It cannot be known through our own thinking or efforts. It can only be known through a special revelation by God.

Second, Romans demonstrates the *reception* of this righteousness—it is received by faith. It cannot be earned. It is a gift of God's grace.

## THE BASIC OUTLINE OF THE BOOK

The simplest outline of the book of Romans divides it into three main parts. It is easy to recognize these divisions because the subject matter changes abruptly.

The first section is a great doctrinal treatise that forms the foundation and basis of the book. It discusses the subjects of sin, justification, and sanctification.

The second section explains how these doctrines are related to the Old Testament, especially to the promises God made to Israel. It shows the sovereignty of God in choosing and working with that nation. It is a dispensational section.

The third section shows how the righteousness of God is to be demonstrated in the lives of believers. It defines their duty to the Lord.

We may chart the book in the following way:

The Book of Romans: The Revelation of God's Righteousness.

DOCTRINE (1–8)
DISPENSATION (9–11)
DUTY (12–16)

## AN ANALYSIS OF THE FIRST SECTION

In studying any book of the Bible, one should look carefully for its logical divisions. It is wrong to try to force the contents into an arbitrary outline. After the main sections have been established, it is then important to determine the subdivisions.

The subject of the first section of Romans is a statement and explanation of the theme. There is also a large subdivision that shows the need for God's revelation of his righteousness in the Gospel. The reason for this revelation is that "the wrath of God is revealed from heaven against all ungodliness and unrighteousness of men" (Romans 1:18). In other words, all people, collectively and individually, are sinners. This is explained in Romans 1:1–3:20.

The glorious provision God has made to redeem sinners is the doctrine of justification. It is only through the death of Jesus Christ that God can be both "just, and the justifier of him who believes in Jesus" (Romans 3:26). The nature, provision, and illustration of justification are given in Romans 3:21–5:21.

The last subdivision of this section concerns the doctrine of sanctification. Although there is confusion about this subject today, the apostle Paul shows how it is possible for the believer to live a life of holiness. It is done only in the power of the Holy Spirit. This is explained in chapters 6–8.

A logical grouping of this material is as follows:

PART ONE: DOCTRINE (1–8)

The Doctrine of Sin (1:1–3:20)

The Doctrine of Justification (3:21–5:21)

The Doctrine of Sanctification (6:1–8:39)

## AN ANALYSIS OF THE SECOND SECTION

An important and unanswered question in the minds of Paul's hearers' had to do with how the doctrines of justification and sanctification related to the Old Testament promises given to the nation Israel. Had God not promised this people to be a nation? Had God not given this people covenants? Had God not chosen this people for himself? How could God offer a salvation based wholly and only on faith? What is the relationship of these New Testament truths to the Old Testament promises?

The apostle Paul gives a clear answer to these questions in three crucial chapters. In chapter 9 he traces the history of Israel. God chose to work with the entire nation, but the promises went only to those who believed in him. In chapter 10 he shows that God's message now is to both Jew and Gentile, that "whoever will call upon the name of the Lord will be saved" (Romans 10:13). It is still by faith. In chapter 11 he describes the glorious future of this nation. One day the people as a nation will turn to the Lord by faith. There is no conflict between what God promised in the Old Testament and what God presents in Romans.

This section may be summarized as follows:

PART TWO: DISPENSATION (9–11)

Israel, Its Past (9)
Israel, Its Present (10)
Israel, Its Future (11)

## AN ANALYSIS OF THE THIRD SECTION

Having explained how God declares sinners righteous on the basis of Christ's death and enables them to live for God, Paul goes on to explain how righteousness is to be demonstrated in the lives of believers.

The service of believers to God, to other believers, and to non-believers is described in chapters 12 and 13. Principles for disputed things are given in 14:1–15:13. The epistle concludes with Paul's personal testimony in a practical demonstration of the righteousness God gives (15:14–16:27).

These subdivisions may be seen as follows:

Part Three: Duty (12–16)
- The Duty in Service (12:1–13:14)
- The Duty Concerning Disputed Issues (14:1–15:13)
- The Duty of Paul (15:14–16:27)

## THE IMPORTANCE OF BIBLE DOCTRINE

The entire Bible is not a textbook of doctrine, nor does it claim to be. Each book of the Bible is written for the specific purpose disclosed within it. But as we have already seen, the expressed purpose of the book of Romans is to teach Bible doctrine. It is probably the most doctrinal book of Scripture.

*Doctrine* has fallen into disrepute today because of ridicule from those who do not believe the Word of God. But most have some doctrinal understanding, whether accurate or inaccurate, whether of God or of man. However, it is possible to gain true doctrinal understanding only through a careful study of the Word of God. This is what the apostle meant when he spoke about learning "sound" or "healthy" doctrine (Titus 1:9, 2:1).

There are several reasons why we need to know the doctrines of the Bible, including the doctrines of the book of Romans. First, doctrine is the only way our faith can be *defined*. It is important to be precise in the content of our faith, and this comes from a doctrinal understanding. For this reason Paul is very particular in defining such doctrines as justification and sanctification.

Second, an understanding of Bible doctrine is important for the *defense* of our faith. Only as we know what we believe can we discern what not to believe. Because we know what our faith is, we also know what it is not.

Third, it is important to know Bible doctrine in order to effectively *distribute* our faith. The motivation to propagate the Gospel of Jesus Christ lies in the knowledge of our human need and the provision God has made to meet it. Sinners can accept this provision and be declared righteous in God's sight only when they are shown what God has done for them.

Perhaps the most important reason to study Bible doctrine is to gain an ability to *demonstrate* our faith. The teaching of the Word of God is the only right foundation for holy daily living. Before believers can live righteously before the Lord, they must know what the Lord expects. Before there can be action, there must be a foundation for that action. This is the method of the book of Romans.

With this overall view of the book, we are ready to look more closely into its various sections.

2

# *Are the Heathen Lost?*

*1:1–32*

"Who changed the truth of God into a lie, and worshipped and served the creature more than the Creator" (Romans 1:25).

---

## THE PROLOGUE (1:1–17)

The opening chapter of Romans begins with the apostle's own introduction to the entire book. He tells who he is, his call of the Lord, and his personal desire to see these believers of whom he has heard. His purpose is to instruct them in the message of the Gospel. But first he shows them that they, and indeed all mankind, have an absolute and unqualified need for redemption. The section may be outlined as follows:

PART ONE: DOCTRINE (1–8)

THE DOCTRINE OF SIN (1:1–3:20)

A. The Prologue (1:1–17)
   1. The Apostle's Salutation (1:1–7)
   2. The Apostle's Stewardship (1:8–16)
   3. The Apostle's Statement of Purpose (1:17)

B. The Heathen Are Guilty Before God (1:18–32)
   1. The Knowledge Revealed (1:18–20)
   2. The Knowledge Rejected (1:21–23)
   3. The Consequences of the Rejection (1:24–32)

### 1. The Apostle's Salutation (1:1–7)

The first word of this epistle denotes not only Paul's authorship of the book, but also that he was acting as the minister of God to the Gentiles. Paul had a double name, *Saulos Paulos*, as many did during that time, and this gave him access to both Jews and Greeks. When he began to turn to the Gentiles, he was presented to them under his Greek name, *Paulos*, which he had possessed as a second name all along. This name is first used in Acts when he turns to the Gentiles (Acts 13:9). There is no question that he is speaking to Gentiles in Romans.

In the opening verse he relates himself to the Lord he serves, to his apostolic office, and to the ministry God has set before him. With the word *servant* ("slave"), he describes himself as the property of the one he serves. It is used of Christ himself to emphasize his obedience to the death of the cross (Philippians 2:7) and is applicable to all who claim the name of Christ. It was because Paul was a slave of Jesus Christ that he was a minister to Roman believers.

Paul was an apostle because he was called by God. Although the word *apostle* means "one who is sent forth," an apostle in the New Testament sense was one who had seen the risen Lord and was especially gifted by God to establish the church (1 Corinthians 9:1; Ephesians 2:20). The God-given ministry of this apostle was the proclamation of the Gospel.

The Gospel Paul preached did not originate in the empty Greek philosophy of his day. It had been anticipated by the Old Testament prophets, and it centered on a person. The uniqueness of Jesus Christ as the Savior of the world was in the fact that he had to be both man and God. He had to be man (v. 3) to die, because God cannot die. And he had to be God (v. 4) to be victorious over death. He was willing and able to die for our sins. Moreover, his resurrection showed his deity. Christ did not become the Son of God through the resurrection (cf. Psalm 2:7). He was raised from the dead because he was the Son of God. His death and the meaning of it is the Gospel, and this is what Paul preached.

The grace of God is the favor he offers to those who don't deserve it and cannot earn it. Besides redeeming people through grace, God also calls believers to service through grace (v. 5). Paul received his call to service from the Lord. Because of God's grace, he was privileged to be the minister to the Gentiles and therefore to the believers at Rome.

It is interesting that this book is not addressed to the "church of Rome" but to "all that be in Rome" (v. 7). There was no central organization at this time. The people simply met in homes. The book is addressed to the believers there, those who were called, those beloved of God, those who were saints. Even though they needed instruction in the Christian way of life, they, like all believers, had a perfect position before the Lord.

This, Paul's longest book, uses his standard (except for 1 and 2 Timothy) greeting: grace and peace. Grace is the unmerited favor of God, giving salvation to all who accept it, even though they don't deserve it. Peace is the cessation of hostility, especially concerning the wrath of God, with subsequent peace of mind. Although many today are looking for peace, only through God can true peace come.

### 2. The Apostle's Stewardship (1:8–16)

These verses give a glimpse of Paul's personal love and concern for those to whom he wrote. Since the apostle was the minister to the Gentiles, it was natural to question why he had never been to Rome, the central city of the Gentiles.

Paul answers this important question by instructing the believers there in his concept of the ministry: Spiritual service does not always mean outward activity. Although he had not as yet traveled to Rome, he had prayed for the believers there. Paul believed that everything should be done as an act of worship to the Lord, including unceasing prayer on their behalf. His prayer was for God to take him to Rome. Little did he realize how this prayer would ultimately be answered. When he did finally visit Rome, he was in chains.

The reason Paul wanted to see these believers was to establish them in the faith. The believers at Rome did not have a well-organized church and there was no central authority. Furthermore, they were neglecting to use spiritual gifts, such as the gifts of apostles, prophets, evangelists, and pastor-teachers (Ephesians 4:11). Paul's purpose in visiting would be to give apostolic leadership, to encourage them to exercise the gifts God had given, and to establish them on a solid foundation in the teachings of the Christian faith. And the believers would provide great comfort and fellowship to Paul. Until that time, however, they would be instructed by this letter.

Paul had wanted to visit these believers on several different occasions, but each time he had been prevented from doing so. What continued to drive him on?

One reason he wanted to visit Rome was to have fruit there as he did among other nations. But another reason was his obligation to preach the Gospel. This is expressed in verses 14–16, where the phrase "I am" occurs three times.

When Paul said "I am debtor" (v. 14), he divided the world into two major divisions. Any language other than Greek was considered barbaric. Any people who were not wise were foolish. So Paul was emphasizing the fact that he was a debtor to the entire world, a world divided on the basis of both language and culture.

The reason he was a debtor is especially significant. It was because he had received a gift of God, his gift of apostleship. He was not only saved, he was also called of God. He was obligated to God and therefore a debtor to the world. All believers are also debtors to whatever God has called them to do.

An outgrowth of this obligation was that Paul was ready (v. 15). This meant that he was prepared by his background and education. But in particular he was ready because this was the purpose of God for which he had been called. He was ready to preach the gospel to those at Rome.

The last "I am" is negative: "I am not ashamed" (v. 16). Everything that humans touch, all that they make, all that they see, will eventually fail. God has said that "the world passes away" (1 John 2:17).

People concerned only with this world will certainly be disappointed. New products deteriorate. Old problems seemingly have no solution. The world is falling apart at the seams, and human solutions cannot hold it together.

But it is different with Paul because it is different with the Gospel of Christ. The apostle need never be ashamed because the Gospel works every time. It is the power (*dunamis*, that which results from an internal force) of God unto salvation. All who believe will be saved. Paul need never worry about that. The power is in the Gospel and is released to all who believe.

Historically, the Jewish people believed first. This was God's method throughout the book of Acts. The Gospel was proclaimed to the Jews first on the day of Pentecost (Acts 2), on the island of Cyprus (Acts 13:5), and even in Thessalonica (Acts 17:1–2). The Jews had the Gospel by precedence but not priority. Both Jew and Gentile are one in the body of Christ (Ephesians 3:5–6), and therefore Paul's obligation is equally to both (Romans 1:14–15). The Jews received the Gospel first out of the mercy, grace, and longsuffering of God.

### 3. The Apostle's Statement of Purpose (1:17)

This verse explains Paul's purpose for writing Romans: to reveal the righteousness of God. This is the righteousness God gives sinners so that they meet God's demands for righteousness. This gives believers a perfect standing in God's sight. This is what is revealed in the Gospel, and this is what the book of Romans teaches.

Moreover, the revelation of this righteousness is from faith to faith; that is, it is all of faith and not of works.

This theme is not limited to the book of Romans. It also occurs in other books of Scripture, with different emphases. The Old Testament quotation "the just shall live by his faith" (Habakkuk 2:4) is repeated three times in the New Testament, each time giving the theme of the book in which it occurs.

The emphases, themes, and references are as follows:

THE JUST shall live by faith (Romans 1:17).

The just SHALL LIVE by faith (Galatians 3:11).

The just shall live BY FAITH (Hebrews 10:38).

The theme of Romans is the righteousness of God. The theme of Galatians is the life in God, and the theme of Hebrews is the life in faith.

## THE HEATHEN ARE GUILTY BEFORE GOD (1:18–32)

The Gospel reveals the righteousness of God because people need to have this righteousness. The Lord does not make righteous people righteous. He makes sinners righteous. People must realize they are lost before they can be saved. Thus, the apostle deals with the subject of sin in the first three chapters of Romans. All mankind is sinful, collectively and individually. To show the universality of sin, Paul divides mankind into three groups. He then marches each before the court of God, marshals the evidence against them, and shows that all stand condemned before God. These groups are the heathen (Romans 1:18–32), the good people (2:1–16), and the religious people (2:17–3:8). A summary is then given showing that all mankind is sinful (Romans 3:9–20).

### 1. The Knowledge Revealed (1:18–20)

God revealed his righteousness in the Gospel because he was also revealing his wrath (v. 18). People are not ignorant of God's attitude toward sin. They know of both God's wrath and righteousness in the religious sphere and in the moral sphere. Both of these areas show mankind to be helpless and hopeless before God's wrath. Although they knew about the wrath of God toward sin, they continued living in unrighteousness. Thus they rejected the truth.

God reveals himself to mankind from within them and, through nature, from without.

Nature reveals God's eternal power and Godhead (v. 20), although it does not explain his relationship to mankind. His power is displayed throughout the universe: creation, sustenance, government (Colossians 1:16–17; Hebrews 1:3). His Godhead, or perhaps better, his Godhood, manifests his deity. God is not a part of mankind. The greatness and detail of creation shows his omnipotence and omniscience. The vast universe must have been brought into existence by one who was very powerful. The intricate design of every aspect of this universe shows the intelligence of the one who brought it into existence. Natural revelation shows that God exists and can be clearly seen by all. The purpose of this revelation is to make it impossible for anyone to plead ignorance of God.

### 2. The Knowledge Rejected (1:21–23)

The universal willful rejection of God's revelation of himself is seen in history. God revealed, but humans willfully rejected; they would not receive God's revelation. Moreover, humanity became vain in their own imagination and professed themselves to be all-wise. Furthermore, they did not glorify God, but changed his glory by making him into images that looked like them and even like animals that were beneath them. In other words, humans attempted to deify themselves and in so doing degraded their concept of the nature of God.

### 3. The Consequences of the Rejection (1:24–32)

Although some accept an evolutionary theory of human origin, there is no evidence in Scripture for such a view. There is also no evidence to support the idea of moral improvement through self-efforts. Scripture unapologetically describes humans as being completely regressed. Because of people's rejection of God's revelation, God gave them up.

The phrase "God gave them up" or "God gave them over" is found three times in these remaining verses of chapter 1 (vv. 24, 26, 28). It indicates that God allowed the people to continue in their immoral ways and no longer urged them to change to avoid judgment.

The human body is directly affected by the way people live. It becomes dishonored as a natural outcome when we indulge our lusts. When we unrestrainedly practice sin, our affections or emotions are also affected (v. 26). That which God gave to express love, peace, and joy is perverted so that it expresses gross immorality. And our minds become filled with all unrighteousness when we live in sin (v. 28).

As people are composed of body, emotion, and intellect, all of these are affected by the rejection of God. By turning from what God said, we regress to our own lusts, vile affections, and all unrighteousness.

This is not a sin done in ignorance. These people are aware of the judgment of God. They know that those who commit such things are worthy of death (v. 32). But this does not stop them. Paul concludes that they "... not only do the same, but have pleasure in them that do them" (Romans 1:32). To them such sin may be fun or bring them temporary enjoyment. But such pleasure is superficial, shortlived, and soon will be judged by God. It is only through Jesus Christ that there can be true peace, a pleasure that endures (Romans 5:1).

Without question, these sinners stand condemned in God's sight. They are without excuse. They rejected God's revelation and lived accordingly.

All mankind, collectively and individually, body, emotion, and mind, are guilty in God's sight. They "have sinned, and come short of the glory of God" (Romans 3:23). These know that "the wages of sin is death" (Romans 6:23). If mankind is to be saved at all, salvation must come by means of another.

# 3

# *Universality of Sin*

*2:1–3:20*

> "For all have sinned" (Romans 3:23)

---

## THE GOOD PEOPLE ARE GUILTY BEFORE GOD (2:1–16)

The book of Romans presents the revelation of God's righteousness and his wrath toward unrighteousness. The heathen stand guilty before God because they have rejected the revelation in nature that God provided. But what about good, moral people? What about those who are socially acceptable? And what about religious people?

What about those who are sincere in their beliefs and devoted to their religion?

Paul divides mankind into three major groups: heathen, good people, and religious people. After giving evidence against each group, he shows why God pronounces them guilty. This section concludes with a summary of universal sin, "there is none righteous, no, not one" (Romans 3:10).

It may be outlined as follows:

PART ONE: DOCTRINE (1–8)

The Doctrine of Sin (1:1–3:20)

- A. The Prologue (1:1–17)
- B. The Heathen Are Guilty Before God (1:18–32)
- C. The Good People Are Guilty Before God (2:1–16)
  - 1. The Principles of God's Judgment (2:1)
    - a. Truth (2:2–5)
    - b. Works (2:6–10)
    - c. Impartiality (2:11–16)
- D. The Religious People Are Guilty Before God (2:17–3:8)
  - 1. The Pride of The Jew (2:17–20)
  - 2. The Practice of The Jew (2:21–24)
  - 3. The Praise of The Jew (2:25–29)
  - 4. The Profit of The Jew (3:1–8)
- E. All Are Guilty Before God (3:9–20)
  - 1. All Are Sinners (3:9–12)
  - 2. Every Part of Us Is Sinful (3:13–18)
  - 3. The Whole World Is Guilty Before God (3:19–20)

### 1. The Principles of God's Judgment (2:1)

Chapter 3 begins with a pronouncement of judgment on those who would judge the heathen for rejecting God's truth. The heathen were definitely wrong because they repressed and would not receive God's revelation. But those judging them, the self-righteous moralizers, were no better than those they presumed to judge. It was true that the heathen had not *received* the truth, but those who judged them had not *responded* to the truth. The heathen would not accept the Word, but the people who accepted it did not apply it to themselves. Both the heathen and moralizers were guilty before God.

***a. Truth (2:2–5)***

There is a vast difference between the way God judges and the way humans judge. God said, "For my thoughts are not your thoughts, neither are your ways my ways" (Isaiah 55:8). In other words, whatever we think and whatever we do is not what God thinks or does. And this relates to judgment. We evaluate the outward appearance, but God looks on the heart. We cannot judge others rightly because we cannot judge ourselves rightly. But God can. And God's judgment is according to certain important principles.

One principle of God's judgment is that it is according to truth, that which is real. We can be certain God will judge fairly because of his nature. God is the God of truth (John 17:3; 1 John 5:20), and his judgment will be in accordance with the truth.

In spite of this, these people tried to reason their way out from under the judgment of God. They made two major errors, both of which the apostle answers. First, they thought their own self-righteousness would allow them to escape the judgment of God (v. 3). This was absolutely wrong. For if God judged the heathen for rejecting his revelation, he would have to judge moralizers for not applying his revelation. Although their sin was different, the results were exactly the same.

Their second error was in thinking that the delay in God's judgment meant they would escape it (v. 4). This thinking was not only fuzzy, it was faulty. It was true that

God had delayed his judgment, but not so they would escape it. God delayed his judgment to bring them to repentance. The goodness and graciousness of God was meant to soften their hearts and lead them to himself.

But what did these people do with the longsuffering of God? Instead of coming to repentance, they despised him. They refused his goodness. They hardened their hearts and therefore stored up the wrath of God until the day they would be judged (vv. 4–5).

*b. Works (2:6–10)*

Another way God judges is according to peoples' deeds. This does not mean that faith is overlooked or ignored. Instead, it shows that God's righteous judgment looks at the results as well as the process. James said, "Faith without works is dead [barren]" (James 2:20). By this he meant that outward works indicate inward faith. A righteous judgment must reveal the truth as well as the deeds or results.

The works of these good people showed that they did not apply God's revelation. Many of the judgments of Scripture have works as as basis for indicating faith (Matthew 25:40; Revelation 20:12–13). According to this criteria, these people will be judged righteously and found guilty.

The contrast between those who obey God's revelation and those who do not is apparent in their works. As a result of trusting God, some will continue in well-doing and receive glory, honor, and immortality (v. 7). These are qualities that humans lack. They belong to Christ alone (John 17:5, 22; Revelation 5:12; 1 Timothy 6:16; 1 John 5:11–12). Others know the truth but disobey it. They do not apply it to themselves. These who obey unrighteousness will receive the judgment of God (v. 8). The good man is headed for judgment as surely as the heathen. Salvation is the work of God. Judgment is the result of the work of man.

***c. Impartiality (2:11–15)***

A third principle of God's judgment is that it cannot be partial; that is, he must judge all of mankind by the law they possess. For instance, the heathen did not have the law of Moses, as did the Jews. But this did not excuse the heathen from being judged. Although they did not have the Mosaic Law, they did have the revelation of God, both externally in nature and internally in their consciences. The revelation of God through nature is emphasized in chapter 1, the result of which is "they are without excuse" (Romans 1:20). Here the fact is presented that they have God's moral law within them, as well as a conscience that bears witness to such a moral law (v. 15). Without question, they have God's revelation both without and within, and must be judged according to what they have.

The Jew, on the other hand, also has a law, but it is a more complete revelation of the mind of God than is found in nature and conscience. The Jew has the Mosaic Law and therefore will be judged according to it. Both the heathen and the Jew are judged on the basis of what they possess (v. 12). It is only in this way that God's judgment is without partiality.

The word *Gentiles* (vv. 14, 24) appears frequently in Romans. It is used to refer to all unbelievers who are not Jews or to the godless peoples of the world. The word *heathen* may be readily substituted in this context. These are the people the apostle speaks of in chapter 1, with whom he contrasts humanly good people in this passage.

The conscience (v. 15) gives knowledge of sin but cannot forgive sin. It is something within us that testifies to right and wrong. Although it can become calloused and hardened, it does give some knowledge of sin similar to the way in which the Mosaic Law showed Israel her sin.

It is taught throughout the Scriptures that God will one day judge the world (Genesis 18:25; 1 Samuel 2:10; Psalm 9:7–8; Isaiah 2:4; Joel 3:12). But the fact that he will judge it through Jesus Christ is spoken only in the New Testament (v. 16; cf. John 5:22). This was the basis of Paul's preaching. He preached not only salvation, but also judgment.

## THE RELIGIOUS PEOPLE ARE GUILTY BEFORE GOD (2:17–3:8)

### 1. The Pride of the Jew (2:17–20)

The apostle cites evidence against different groups of people: the heathen and the morally good. He now turns to the last group, the religious people, who supposedly were closest to God. As an example he uses the Jews, who thought they were the most religious of all the peoples of the earth. Certainly if anyone could claim righteousness before God, it would be the religious people. After all, would not God reward their sincerity and devotion?

The Jews had many privileges the Gentiles did not have. They also had greater responsibility. These privileges, which were the pride of the Jew, are emphasized by the apostle, starting with the fact that the Jews were called Jews, a name that indicated a national difference (v. 17). They were also a separated people, called and chosen by God. They also trusted in the law (v. 17). The Gentiles had a conscience, but the Jews had the Mosaic

Law, a more complete revelation from God. They could claim something the Gentiles did not possess.

The Jews also gloried in God (v. 17). It was the Lord who had acted on their behalf, who had delivered them from Egypt and brought them into the land of Palestine.

The Jews also knew the will of God (v. 18). The prophets had proclaimed divine will to them. They knew what God expected of them, both positively and negatively. Being instructed out of the law they gave approval to the things that excelled (v. 18).

The result of these privileges was that Jews were superior in a number of ways (vv. 19–20). They were guides to the blind. They were the disciplinarians of the foolish. They were teachers of babes. And they had the resemblance of knowledge and truth. They had a superior position: guide, light, instructor, and teacher of others. They had greater privileges. But with this came a greater responsibility.

### The Practice of the Jew (2:21–24)

If this is what the Jews had, what did they do with it? How did they regard these special privileges? Paul now asks five questions. Each one implies an affirmative answer, thereby proving the Jews' guilt. Paul shows that the Jews did not practice what they preached. For instance, they were to teach others, but they did not teach themselves. They preached that no one should steal, but they themselves stole. They preached that no one should commit adultery, but did so themselves. They claimed to detest idols, but they stole them from the heathen shrine for profit. They prided themselves on having the law from God, but broke it at every point. In fact, their disobedient blasphemy of the name of God was even seen by the

Gentiles (v. 24). Although possessing the law, they did not observe it; instead, they disobeyed it in every way.

### 3. The Praise of the Jew (2:25–29)

The Jews, however, did feel they had a privileged position before God. After all, they were part of God's chosen nation. They reasoned that since they had been circumcised, they had a favored relationship with God. They rested in their rite of circumcision. As members of the covenant nation, they believed they would be excused from the judgment of God.

But circumcision, as given in the Old Testament, was not in itself a sign of justification before God. It was a sign of the Abrahamic Covenant, the blessings of which depended on faith and obedience to God (Genesis 12:1–3; 17:10; 23–25). Therefore, the rite of circumcision without the reality of obedience was actually unrighteousness. The Jews could not escape the judgment of God through circumcision. This was only possible through obedience to the law, the revelation God had given them.

But Paul goes a step further. What would happen if uncircumcised Gentiles kept the revelation God gave them? He answers that such ones would be blessed by God. He says, "And shall not uncircumcision which is by nature [the Gentile], if it fulfil the law [the law of conscience God has given him], judge you [the Jew, even though circumcised], who by the letter and circumcision transgresses the law?" (Romans 2:27). Obedience to God's revelation enables one to escape God's judgment. This comes only by faith. All who transgress God's law, including the Jew, are guilty before him.

The praise of Jews is not in their circumcision, but in their obedience to the law of God (v. 29). It is a matter of the heart, not of the flesh; an attitude of faith, not of circumcision. What counts before God, whether one is a Jew or a Gentile, is obedience to the revelation God has given.

### 4. The Profit of the Jew (3:1–8)

It was true that the Jews' relationship to God did not depend on the act of circumcision, but on their faith. It was true that Jews as well as Gentiles were guilty before God. It was true that both had rejected the revelation God had given them. The Gentiles had rejected natural revelation and the Jews had rejected the law. But the Jews did have several advantages, some of which are described here and others of which are discussed in chapters 9–11.

The profit in being a Jew is indicated by three significant questions asked by the apostle (vv. 1, 3, 5). These questions were already in his readers' minds because they thought the Jews had a more favored position toward God than did the Gentiles. But Paul points out that although the Jewish people were favored by God, the Jews also were guilty before God. Jew and Gentile alike stood condemned before God because both had revelation from him and both had rejected it.

The first question (v. 1) concerns what has happened to the privileges of the nation Israel. The fact that Paul uses the plural pronoun *them* (v. 2) shows that this is a reference to the nation Israel rather than to individual Jews. As individuals, many did not believe. But as a nation, they did have privileges.

The particular advantage mentioned is the oracles or utterances of God (v. 2). These included the Mosaic Law given on Mount Sinai, the words of the prophets, and the promises of the Messiah. All of these came through the nation Israel, and the nation received distinctive blessing from God. This blessing continued in spite of individual Jewish unbelief.

The second question (v. 3) concerns the effect, if any, that the unbelief of individual Jews had on the promises of God to Israel. Some wanted to know if the fact that many Jews did not believe would cancel the promises God had made to this nation. The answer is absolutely not!

Several times in this epistle Paul uses the expression "God forbid" (*me genoito*, v. 4). This is a Greek idiom that expresses horror that something is even mentioned. A paraphrase would be, "Horrors! How could you even suggest such a thing!" To suggest that God would not keep his promises blasphemes the very nature of God. God is true and faithful and will fulfill all that he has promised.

God is not only righteous in keeping his promises, but he is also righteous in judging unbelievers. Such judgment was predicted in the promises of God. It was David who said that God was just in judging his sin (v. 4; cf. Psalm 51:4). And God is just in judging all unbelievers. Unbelief does not remove the promises. Rather, it brings judgment on the unbelievers.

The third question (v. 5) concerns what many others have asked. It is a question that attempts to cast doubt on the judgment of God. The question is, "Why should a person be judged for sin if that sin proves God righteous? After all, doesn't this give people a free license to sin?"

Again Paul uses the idiom "God forbid" (v. 6). The ultimate outcome of such faulty reasoning is that God would not have to judge the entire world. This would indeed be unrighteous, and a righteous God cannot act unrighteously. As for those who think they have a license to sin, they also must be judged (v. 8). The Christian life is not one of freedom to do whatever we want to do. It is freedom to do whatever God wants us to do. The freedom, therefore, is not to sin but to obey the revelation of God.

God is just. Jew and Gentile, heathen and religious, "good" and bad all stand guilty before him.

## ALL ARE GUILTY BEFORE GOD (3:9–20)

### 1. All Are Sinners (3:9–12)

The verdict of God is clear. After dividing mankind into three groups and marshalling the evidence against each, the conclusion is that all are under God's decree of sin (v. 9). Because of our disobedience in rejecting the truth, we stand guilty and condemned before God.

This is also the verdict of the Scriptures. The apostle quotes from Psalm 14:1–3 to show the universality of sin (vv. 10–12). None are righteous, none understand, none seek after God, none do good. Universally, humans have nothing in and of themselves that merits the goodness of God. Instead of accepting God's revelation, we rejected it; instead of applying God's revelation we disobeyed it. We stand condemned. Salvation cannot come by human effort.

### 2. Every Part of Us Is Sinful (3:13–18)

All are sinners, and every part of us is sinful. As a physician makes an examination before giving a diagnosis, so Paul gives a spiritual examination to show the manifestation of sin in every part of our lives. He looks at the throat, tongue, lips, mouth, feet, and eyes. He finds that sin has affected every aspect of our nature. Quoting from Psalm 5:9; 140:3; 10:7; Isaiah 59:7–8; and Psalm

36:1, he describes sin in such phrases as "open sepulchre," "deceit," "poison," "cursing and bitterness," "swift to shed blood," "destruction and misery," no way of peace, and "no fear of God" (vv. 13–18). These are the symptoms of the problem of sin visible throughout our natures in our words, deeds, and thoughts. We are condemned sinners before God.

### 3. The Whole World Is Guilty Before God (3:19–20)

The apostle applies these verses to the entire world, because the whole world, Gentile and Jew, is guilty before God. The Jews thought they had a right to judge the Gentiles and did so. But the Jews were also judged by the law God had given to them. So both Gentile and Jew stood condemned before God.

The purpose of the Mosaic Law was not to produce salvation. This was the misconception of the Jew (v. 20). Jews thought that if they kept the law, they would be justified in the sight of God. But this was not true because they could not keep the law. The purpose of the law was to *show* what sin was; it could not *solve* the problem: The law was not a savior. It was a standard showing what God demanded. It was insufficient to save them from their hopeless and helpless state of sin.

In looking back over this lesson, we can see that we all stand guilty in God's sight—unable to save ourselves and unable to find salvation in another person or even in the law God has given. If we are to be justified at all, we must be given righteousness by the one who is both willing and able to do so.

4

# What Is Justification?

*3:21–4:25*

"But as many as received him, to them gave he power to become the sons of God" (John 1:12).

---

## THE DESCRIPTION OF JUSTIFICATION (3:21–31)

The last section of chapter 3 may be called the heart of the book of Romans. Because of its significance, it is important to review the apostle's major thesis. Paul began by pointing out that the Gospel of Jesus Christ revealed God's provision for our righteousness. This was obtained only by faith.

But before we can be saved, we must see that we are lost; before we can be accepted by God, we must see that we are guilty before him. This is why the apostle goes into such detail to show that everyone and all parts of everyone are sinful. Before he can show God's answer to the sin problem, he must show our need of an answer from God. We are lost. If we are to be saved at all, if we are to be acceptable to God, if we are to be righteous, God must provide the way.

The apostle has clearly shown that we are lost. But what has God done to deliver us from our sin? What has God done to make us righteous and acceptable to him? How can a sinner be righteous in the sight of God? This, of course, is what the world is asking. As the crime rate increases, the world sees that sin is very real. God has the answer to the sin problem, and it is the only answer that works. This lesson may be outlined as follows:

PART ONE: DOCTRINE (1–8)
- THE DOCTRINE OF SIN (1:1–3:20)
- THE DOCTRINE OF JUSTIFICATION (3:21–5:21)
  - A. The Description of Justification (3:21–31)
    1. The Channel of Justification (3:21–23)
    2. The Basis of Justification (3:24–26)
    3. The Law and Justification (3:27–31)
  - B. The Illustration of Justification (4:1–25)
    1. The Illustration of Abraham (4:1–8)
    2. The Illustration of Circumcision (4:9–12)
    3. The Illustration of Heirship (4:13–16)
    4. The Illustration of Faith (4:17–25)

### 1. The Channel of Justification (3:21–23)

This great section opens with the word *but*, a conjunction that shows contrast. All that has gone before is now contrasted with the provision God has made. All the benefits God had given during Old Testament times are now contrasted with what he has provided in "the fulness of the time" (Galatians 4:4).

It is the righteousness of God that is now manifested through the Gospel of Jesus Christ. The word *righteousness* is an all-inclusive term. It means "rightness" or "the state of being right." Sometimes it refers to God's character. But in the book of Romans it most often refers to the rightness of man, his state of being right with God. As such, it includes much more than the forgiveness of sins. It involves giving the believer a position before God and a conduct of life in keeping with that position. It is making a believer right before God.

God gives the righteousness no law could give. Gentiles as well as Jews had realized the importance of the law. Jews had trusted in the Mosaic Law and had regarded the keeping of it as their way of life. But Gentiles, on the other hand, had the law of God written on their hearts. They knew from their inner being the morality of God. Even during Old Testament times, the writers of Scripture declared mankind's need for God's righteousness.

This righteousness is received by faith. It is unto all and upon all that believe (v. 22). The problem is one of acceptance, not race or background. God has made the provision. We must accept it by faith. It is not of works, only of faith.

All people live by one of two principles: that of works or that of faith. Those who follow the works principle live by self-reliance, self-confidence, and self-determination. Its motive is the need to "do" something. The other way is that of faith. It is to accept the provision God has made.

God's righteousness is accepted by faith, not earned by works.

The need for this righteousness is universal. It is for all because all have sinned and are continually coming short of the glory of God (v. 23). Since the need is universal, so is the provision.

**2. The Basis of Justification (3:24–26)**

Justification is an act of God, not of any human. The word *justified* (or *justifier*) occurs four times in this section (vv. 20, 24, 26, 28). The word has two main parts: *just-ified*. The first part means "justice" or "righteousness," the theme of Romans. The rest of the word means "to declare." It is therefore the act of God whereby he declares or pronounces the sinner righteous.

Justification means to be *declared* righteous, not *made* righteous. Justification includes much more than forgiving and removing the condemnation of sin. Justification includes the addition of God's righteousness and on that basis the declaration that the sinner is righteous in God's sight. This is the difference between a human tribunal and a divine judgment. A king may grant a pardon to a criminal, but he cannot grant him the position of one who has never broken the law. But what an earthly king cannot do, God does. God not only pardons the sinner, but he also reinstates the person into the position of one who has not broken the law. God declares the sinner righteous, and grants the person a perfect position before him.

The righteousness of God is free to us. The word translated "freely" (v. 24) is translated "without a cause" in John 15:25. Although salvation as a gift may be free from our viewpoint, it cost God his only Son to provide it.

The word *redemption* means "complete deliverance from the penalty, power, and presence of sin for a price that has already been paid." The price paid was the death of Jesus Christ. The deliverance is given to those who believe. As we are complete sinners, so also the salvation God provides is complete.

God's grace motivated him to provide this divine righteousness. Nothing within us has produced it. It is produced by the spontaneous and unmerited favor of God. God's salvation is free, and it is full, final, and forever.

The word *propitiation* (v. 25) means "satisfaction." We have to be redeemed from sin, and God must be satisfied with the payment. Sinners have sinned against God. They have offended the holiness of God. Christ therefore had to die to satisfy God's holy and righteous demands so sinners could be declared righteous.

Only sinners who come to God on the basis of the death of Christ can be justified.

The word *declare* is used in both verse 25 and 26, showing that God declared his righteousness to those who lived both before and after the cross.

During Old Testament times, the sins of the people were covered by the animal sacrifices they brought to God. Although God saved them, he did so because one day their sins would be taken away by the death of Christ.

It was at the cross that God declared his righteousness for the remission of those sins. The death of Christ provided remission for the sins of all people of all ages.

Consider it from God's standpoint. How can a righteous God declare condemned sinners righteous? It almost seems that he would have to do something wrong to reverse such a judgment. But suppose that God first forgave the sinners and then gave them a righteousness that was acceptable to him. If sinners could be both forgiven and righteous, they could be declared righteous before God. God would then be the justifier of the ungodly. But how could he remain just in doing something like that? The only way this can be done is through the death of Christ, the death that satisfies God and is the basis for our redemption and justification. The purpose of God's provision is that he might be both just and the justifier of those who believe.

### 3. The Law and Justification (3:27–31)

But one further point needs to be stressed. How is such a doctrine to be harmonized with the way God dealt with Israel during Old Testament times? If justification is granted on the basis of faith, what about Israel? Did not God deal with that nation on the basis of works? Or did he deal with it on the basis of faith as well?

The apostle answers the question by showing that both the Law and the Gospel exclude any justification by works. Therefore, justification must have been by faith during Old Testament times (vv. 27–28). This means that Jews have nothing of which to boast, because they are not justified by something that belongs exclusively to them.

God deals with both Jew and Gentile on the same basis, that of justification by faith.

People are declared righteous by faith apart from the works of the Law. The fact is that the law was not given to *solve* the problem of sin; it only *showed* the need of a Savior. But now God has provided the solution through his own Son.

## THE ILLUSTRATIONS OF JUSTIFICATION (4:1–25)

### 1. The Illustration of Abraham (4:1–8)

The fact that justification is by faith alone is an important one, and the apostle now seeks to substantiate the truth taught in the previous chapter. If even one example of justification by works could be found, then all the apostle has said would be false. So Paul seeks to prove that justification during Old Testament times was also by faith.

To prove this point, Paul begins with the father of the faithful, Abraham himself. He chooses Abraham because any Jew would immediately identify with him. Moreover, whatever God did for Abraham, he did for all Jews.

The evidence that Abraham was justified by faith is in the Old Testament. Paul shows from Genesis that Abraham was declared righteous because he believed God (v. 3; cf. Genesis 15:6). There is nothing mentioned here about works he accomplished. Abraham believed God.

The apostle further explains this with the example of a laborer and his wages (vv. 4–5). The laborer receives wages he has earned. They are not of grace. Likewise, if God would give righteousness because a person earned it, it would not be of grace. But Abraham did not receive God's righteousness because he worked for it. He simply believed. He accepted what God provided. God's righteousness therefore came by grace and not by works.

Even the Psalmist David confirmed this important fact (vv. 6–8). If a person is truly righteous before God, that person cannot be charged with sin (Psalm 32:1). Since Abraham believed God, he was given God's righteousness; he had no sin imputed to him. It was only through faith that an Old Testament person could be declared acceptable to God.

### 2. The Illustration of Circumcision (4:9–12)

But wait a minute. If all of this is true, what about the rite of circumcision? For the Jew, this was one of the most important requirements, and it all began with Abraham. Was it not true that Abraham was justified because he was circumcised? And if so, then was he not justified by works, the work of circumcision?

Paul anticipates this problem because it was important to the Jew and also to the apostle's point that justification is by faith, not works. His answer is quite clear. He shows the true purpose of circumcision. Circumcision was not a condition of justification. It was a seal to authenticate what had already taken place. Abraham was therefore justified by faith, not circumcision. Furthermore, there were Gentiles who were justified, although they were not circumcised. Since Abraham is the father of all who believe, justification must have a different basis than circumcision, or it would be for Jews only.

### 3. The Illustration of Heirship (4:13–16)

There is another illustration of justification—the promise made to Abraham. The knowledge that he was to be the heir of the world came to him by faith, not by the Mosaic Law. In fact, the Mosaic Law was not given until many years *after* the promise had been given. It was added to the promise, but did not replace it. The Law never produced blessing as did the promise. Salvation therefore came by faith, as did the promise, not by the Mosaic Law.

### 4. The Illustration of Faith (4:17–25)

An important subject in the book of Romans is justification by faith. This has been the heart of this lesson and this section, but until now faith has not really been defined. But a correct concept of faith is essential to the discussion of the way we are justified, and this passage gives such a definition.

The first ingredient of faith is an object for that faith. And the kind of faith we have depends on the object of our faith. In Abraham's case, he believed God, the God of power, the God who was able to accomplish his purpose. For instance, this God was able to cause the birth of Isaac long after Abraham was reproductively sterile. Another example of the power of God was that he raised Christ from the dead.

But faith is also based on knowledge, the knowledge of the promise of God (v. 21). Abraham believed God in that he knew the promise of God, and he knew that God was able to perform his promise. Faith is not a work; it believes what God has promised as if it had already happened.

Moreover, this is related to all believers because they must be justified on the basis of faith. In fact, throughout the history of the world God has never justified anyone on the basis of works. It is valid to place our faith in Christ for salvation because that is God's only provision.

The finished work of Christ makes all of this possible. What he has done makes justification possible on the faith principle. Although the death of Christ is the basis of justification, the resurrection of Christ shows that every offense against God's holiness has been satisfied. The believer is justified, and it is on the basis of faith alone.

5

# *God's Abounding Grace*

*5:1–21*

> "Therefore being justified by faith, we have peace with God through our Lord Jesus Christ" (Romans 5:1).

---

## THE BENEFITS OF JUSTIFICATION (5:1–11)

Justification by faith is the great teaching of Romans. Condemned sinners, guilty in God's sight, are forgiven. They are given God's righteousness and declared righteous before him. They are now acceptable to God. Their standing before God has been completely changed. This is the marvel of the miracle of God, a work that only God could do. But this provision must be accepted by individuals. It can be given only on the principle of faith.

But if it takes only faith to initiate such a salvation, will it really last? Does justification have such a sure foundation that it will last through the trials and storms of life? In other words, what benefits accrue to the believer who is declared righteous? How is the grace of God manifested in human life?

The apostle Paul is a master teacher. He anticipates important questions and answers them. This is why he discusses the next step, the grace of God in the life of the one justified by God.

This section may be outlined as follows:

PART ONE: DOCTRINE (1–8)

- THE DOCTRINE OF SIN (1:1–3:20)
- THE DOCTRINE OF JUSTIFICATION (3:21–5:21)
  - A. The Description of Justification (3:21–31)
  - B. The Illustrations of Justification (4:1–25)
  - C. The Benefits of Justification (5:1–11)
    1. Peace with God (5:1)
    2. Access to God (5:2a)
    3. Hope in God (5:2b)
    4. Fruit of Tribulation (5:3–4)
    5. Love (5:5a)
    6. The Holy Spirit (5:5b)
    7. Deliverance from God's Wrath (5:6–10)
    8. Joy (5:11)
  - D. The Application of Justification (5:12–21)
    1. The Headship of Adam (5:12–14)
    2. The Contrasts of Adam's and Christ's Headships (5:15–21)

### 1. Peace with God (5:1)

Justification is an act of God whereby he declares people righteous in his sight. It rests on what God has done, not on human attitude or feelings. Justification not only pardons sin, but it also reinstates a person to a right relationship and position before God.

One result of being declared righteous is peace with God. This is not mere tranquility of mind but a cessation of hostility. Since we are sinners, God was our righteous enemy because God hates sin. But when believers are justified, they have peace with God.

Although justification rests on what God has done, some like to substitute other things for faith. Some want to substitute feelings, while others would like to substitute intellect for faith.

This does not mean that feeling and intellect are unimportant, nor does it mean they are not involved with faith. But peace with God is a result of justification that comes by faith alone. A world looking for peace must know that true peace, peace with God, comes only with the removal of guilt in the sight of God.

**2. Access to God (5:2a)**

In Old Testament times, believers could not come directly to God. They had to go through a priest. This was the Levitical system, the system of the Mosaic Law. Believers are no longer under that system. Because of Christ's work on the cross they are declared righteous and have direct access to God.

**3. Hope in God (5:2b)**

Because justification is a work of God, it is complete. It does not have to be done again. The believer can never lose it. In the mind of God the future is as complete as the present or past. The believer can therefore rejoice in the hope of the future and be certain that the hope will be fulfilled.

### 4. Fruit of Tribulation (5:3–4)

Since God will not fail the believer, the question becomes, will the believer's faith fail the Lord? The apostle answers this important question by showing what adversity in life produces in the believer. Believers are to glory in tribulations, because out of them they receive hope and something extra. Tribulation brings patience, and patience produces an added feature: approved character. Some may think tribulation would cause believers to lose faith. Actually, it strengthens it. Trials in the life of the believer produce an approved character. This, in turn, produces hope.

### 5. Love (5:5a)

The apostle points out further that believers' hope is certain of fulfillment and will not put them to shame. Their hope is certain because God has given them a pledge of fulfillment. This pledge is his love which is poured out by the Holy Spirit. If God has given this, he will certainly fulfill the rest.

### 6. The Holy Spirit (5:5b)

The Holy Spirit, mentioned for the first time in this passage, is discussed in greater detail in chapter 8. During this age, whenever people receive God's gift of salvation, they are immediately indwelt by the Holy Spirit (1 Corinthians 6:19). The Spirit of God resides within believers. Part of the Spirit's work is to pour out God's love on them. This is God's pledge that he will accomplish his purpose.

### 7. Deliverance from God's Wrath (5:6–10)

Believers who have been saved from sin have seen the work of God in their lives. But God has also done many things for unbelievers. For instance, "while we were yet sinners, Christ died for us" (Romans 5:8). Christ died for the ungodly, not for the godly.

But if God did all this for his enemies, the ungodly, imagine what he must do for his friends, the believers. If he reconciled sinners unto himself, then he will certainly do something for his friends.

The fact that God has reconciled sinners unto himself means that he will certainly keep the believer. God will bring the believer into his ultimate salvation, the time when the believer will be spared from the wrath of judgment (v. 9) and be eternally united with the Father.

But there is more. The believer will also share in the life of Christ (v. 10). The believer becomes a child of God and possesses God's life.

### 8. Joy (5:11)

The apostle mentions one more benefit that comes to those who have been justified. It is the boast believers will make in Jesus Christ because of all Christ has done for them. Christ has given new life, peace, and fellowship with him. Believers have been reconciled to God through Christ (the word *atonement* should be translated "reconciliation") and enjoy the benefits of being declared righteous.

The results of justification are many; in fact, this is only a partial list. All that believers have is due to their being declared righteous before God by the redemption in Jesus Christ.

## THE APPLICATION OF JUSTIFICATION (5:12–21)

### 1. The Headship of Adam (5:12–14)

The apostle now begins a summary of all that he has taught so far in this book. He contrasts justification with condemnation. Believers stand accepted before God because they are declared righteous in his sight. Sinners stand condemned before God because they are guilty in his sight. As the sinner is guilty in Adam, so the believer is righteous in Christ.

The apostle begins by showing that death has affected all people as a result of the sin of one man, Adam. The last part of verse 12 is quite explicit, "for that all have sinned." The word *all* shows that sin is universal. The word *sinned* is in a tense that denotes completed action in past time. In other words, all were in Adam sinning when he sinned.

There is an illustration of this principle in Hebrews 7. According to this passage, Levi, who lived many years after Abraham, paid tithes to Melchisedec. A careful study of the event shows that it was Abraham who paid tithes to Melchisedec (Genesis 14:20). But the Scripture says that Levi, the great grandson of Abraham, also paid tithes to Melchisedec in that he "paid tithes in Abraham. For he was yet in the loins of his father, when Melchisedec met him" (Hebrews 7:9–10). In the same way, all were in Adam sinning when he sinned and are therefore sinners by nature and participation.

This is further illustrated by the fact that people died before the Mosaic Law was given. Death, therefore, is not the result of the law, but the result of Adam's sin. Abraham, Isaac, and Jacob all died. This is because they were sinners. People die because sin entered the race through Adam's sin.

### 2. The Contrasts of Adam's and Christ's Headships (5:15–21)

But there is another headship, the headship of Christ. Adam was the head of the race, and through him sin permanently entered human life. But Christ is the head of another race, the race that is justified through him. There is similarity in that what each did affects many. But the headships of Adam and Christ are headships of contrast. Christ did the opposite of what Adam did.

One example of this is that although death came upon all people through Adam's sin, the grace of God came upon many through Jesus Christ (v. 15). Condemnation came to all through Adam. But justification came to many by Jesus Christ (v. 16). Through the sin of Adam, death reigned upon all. But the gift of divine righteousness is given by Jesus Christ (v. 17).

The apostle puts these contrasts side by side in his concluding paragraph. Through Adam came condemnation; through Christ came justification. Through Adam many were made sinners; through Christ many were made righteous. Through Adam sin abounded; through Christ grace did much more abound. Through Adam sin reigned unto death; through Christ grace reigned through righteousness.

Medical science has made many advances. One of these is organ transplantation. Eye transplants are somewhat common. In certain instances an eye has been taken from a criminal about to be executed and given to restore someone's sight. When that eye was a part of the criminal, it participated in all that he did. It saw what he wanted to see. When the eye became a part of someone else, it saw what the new owner wanted it to see.

For the sake of illustration, suppose that believers were like that eye. When they were in Adam, they were everything Adam was both by inheritance and by choice. They shared his sin, condemnation, and death. But by the miracle of new birth, divine transplantation, believers are now in Christ. With new will and emotions they now share in all that Christ is. They share in his salvation, justification, and life.

There is no question that Christ has done much more for believers than for unbelievers. In fact, this is what the apostle teaches throughout this chapter. Five times he uses the phrase "much more," and an enumeration of these makes a good summary of this chapter.

They may be listed as follows:

a. The "much more" of justification (v. 9)
b. The "much more" of reconciliation (v. 10)
c. The "much more" of the gift (v. 15)
d. The "much more" of the reign in life (v. 17)
e. The "much more" of abounding grace (v. 20)

# 6

# *Union with Christ*

*6:1–7:25*

"But now being made free from sin" (Romans 6:22).

---

## POSITIONAL SANCTIFICATION (6:1–10)

Having discussed condemnation (1:1–3:20) and justification (3:21–5:21), Paul turns to sanctification (6:1–8:39). The word *sanctify* specifically means "to set apart." The believer is set apart to God from sin (1 Thessalonians 1:9).

Justification is the believer's righteous standing before God. It is God's answer to the question of guilt. But now arises the important question of the life the justified people live. Their *position* is perfect before God, but what about their *condition* or walk before God? Their standing may be perfect, but what about their state?

Sin has not only a penalty that needs to be forgiven, but also a power that needs to be counteracted. The process whereby believers are set apart to God from sin is sanctification.

There are three tenses, or aspects, of sanctification, each related to the others. Since believers have a perfect position before God, they are positionally set apart, or sanctified to God. One day they will be removed from the very essence of sin, but in this present life they must continually deal with sin.

The tenses of sanctification may be outlined as follows:

1. *Positional sanctification.* This happened in the *past*, when believers accepted Christ as personal Savior. At that time they were placed in Christ with a perfect *position* before God. As such, they were delivered from the *penalty* of sin (1 Corinthians 1:2, 30; 6:11; Hebrews 10:10, 14).

2. *Progressive sanctification.* This is what believers experience during the *present*, day by day in their Christian life. They are *progressively* being set apart from the *power* of sin in their lives and unto God (John 17:17; Ephesians 5:26; 1 Thessalonians 4:3; 2 Thessalonians 2:13; 1 Peter 1:2).

3. *Perfect sanctification.* This is what believers will receive in the *future* when they meet the Lord. They will then be *perfect*, in both position and condition, as they stand before God. They will be delivered from the very *presence* of sin (Romans 8:29, 30; Philippians 3:21; 1 John 3:1–2).

The apostle discusses both positional and progressive sanctification in Romans 6 and then shows what happens to those who do not follow his instruction in chapter 7. The section may be outlined as follows:

PART ONE: DOCTRINE (1–8)

The Doctrine of Sin (1:1–3:20)

The Doctrine of Justification (3:21–5:21)

The Doctrine of Sanctification (6:1–8:39)

A. Positional Sanctification (6:1–10)
- Step 1. We Died (6:1–5)
- Step 2. We Know (6:6–10)

B. Progressive Sanctification (6:11–23)
- Step 3. We Reckon (6:11)
- Step 4. We Yield (6:12–17)
- Step 5. We Are Free (6:18–23)

C. Powerless Sanctification (7:1–25)
1. The Marriage of the Saint (7:1–6)
2. The Purpose of the Law (7:7–14)
3. The Struggle of the Saint (7:15–25)

### Step 1. We Died (6:1–5)

Two major questions are raised in this chapter, both of which concern the relationship of the believer to the sin problem: (1) Shall we continue in sin that grace may abound? (v. 1) and (2) Shall we sin because we are not under law but under grace? (v. 15). Both concepts are repudiated, and the apostle teaches believers how to have deliverance from the power of sin.

The question of abounding grace (v. 1) was a natural one because Paul emphasized a gospel of grace, not works. He had said that "where sin abounded, grace did much more abound" (Romans 5:20). But he did not mean by this that believers should continue in sin to demonstrate the grace of God.

The apostle's answer is an untranslatable idiom rendered "God forbid" (v. 2). The actual meaning is "Horrors! How could you even think of such a thing!" The expression occurs several times in Romans.

God's purpose for believers is to produce in them a life of holiness (1 Peter 1:15–16). Although it may seem to be an impossible standard, holiness is God's clear expectation for every one of his children. As he is holy, the believer is also to be holy.

How, then, can believers obtain such a perfect position and attain such a perfect practice in life?

In this chapter the apostle uses five key words to show five steps that will make holiness a reality in believers' lives, if they follow them. These key words of Romans 6 are: *dead* (v. 2); *knowing* (v. 6); *reckon* (v. 11); *yield* (v. 13); *free* (v. 18).

The apostle begins by showing that believers do not need to work to obtain a perfect position before God. They already have it. Believers already have freedom from the rule of sin. They already have positional sanctification. They stand perfect before God.

All believers have within them a capacity to sin. This is called a "sin nature." Believers also have a new divine nature, a capacity to serve God. But until death they continue to have an old nature as well (1 John 1:8). The possession of this old nature gives believers many problems. If there were some way they could gain freedom from it, they would then be free to serve the Lord.

And Paul says that every believer has this freedom from the rule of the sin nature. Believers have died to the sin nature. But the sin nature itself did not die. Even though the sin nature wants the believer to serve it, the apostle says that the believer has died to it.

The word *dead* does not imply annihilation or cessation of existence. When people die physically, they do not cease to exist. Their material nature, the body, is separated from their immaterial nature, the soul. For believers, this is to be "absent from the body and present with the Lord" (2 Corinthians 5:6, 8). And the fact that believers have died to the sin nature means they are separated from it. They are no longer obligated to serve it.

During a recent war a wife asked to have her husband, who had been missing in action, declared legally dead. Although he may or may not have been dead, such legal action separated the wife from her husband so she was no longer obligated to him. In the same way believers have been separated from their sin natures so they no longer have to serve it.

What is the legal action that has separated believers from their sin nature? How is it that they are no longer obligated to serve it?

An important word in this passage is the word *baptized*, a transliteration of the Greek word *baptizo* (v. 3). The same word is used not only of water baptism but also of the baptism of the Holy Spirit, of fire, of Moses, of Jesus, and of John (Luke 3:16; 1 Corinthians 10:2; Luke 3:21; John 4:1). The implication of the word in this passage is "identification," where believers are identified with the death, burial, and resurrection of Christ.

When people accept Christ as Savior, they receive the life of Christ. Moreover, they are identified with all that Christ did, including his death, burial, and resurrection. Since Christ died with respect to the sin nature, so did believers. This is why believers are no longer obligated to serve the sin nature.

#### Step 2. We Know (6:6–10)

When Christ enters people's lives, the power of the sin nature is rendered inoperative. Their co-crucifixion with Christ results in the nullification of that through which the sin nature expresses itself. So believers are no longer obligated to serve sin.

But believers were also raised with Christ that "we also should walk in newness of life" (Romans 6:4). Believers not only died with Christ, but they also united with him (v. 8). Being raised with Christ means that believers are delivered from the bondage of sin and that the sin nature no longer has unquestioned lordship over them.

### PROGRESSIVE SANCTIFICATION (6:11–23)

#### Step 3. We Reckon (6:11)

The position of believers is identification with the death, burial, and resurrection of Christ. Although the believer is free from the condemnation of sin, how can they be free from the control of sin? This is accomplished by believing what has happened and acting in accordance with it.

The word *reckon* (v. 11) means "to count it to be so." Believers are to know and believe their position that they have died to sin and are alive to God. What God has done is a fact, and they are asked to believe this fact. Believers are not asked to establish or prove something, only to believe what has taken place. In fact, they are commanded to do so.

The basis of believers' practice is their position; they are to live a life they already have; they are to become what they are.

Suppose that every day you ate supper at 5:30 and went outside for a walk at 6:30. But one day you made an airplane trip. The plane left at 5:00 and you were served supper at 5:30. At 6:30 you decided to go outside for your usual walk and found you had a problem. And so you learned a very basic spiritual truth, the truth of Romans 6: that you must act according to where you are. You must live according to your position. When you are at home, you act in a certain way, but when you are in an airplane, you act in a different way. Believers who have died to the sin nature are to believe it and to conduct their lives accordingly.

**Step 4. We Yield (6:12–17)**

The word *yield* (v. 13) means "submit," "commit," or "present." The same word is translated "present" in Romans 12:1. Before believers were saved, their bodies were an instrument of sin. Sin expressed itself through their bodies. But they are no longer to yield their members to sin (vv. 12–13a). They are to yield them to God as instruments of righteousness (vv. 13b–17). All that was once used to serve sin is now to be used to serve the Lord.

**Step 5. We Are Free (6:18–23)**

Believers who were once in bondage to sin are now free from that bondage. They are no longer servants of the sin nature. They no longer have to sin.

But the paradox of the Christian life is that although believers are free from sin, they are enslaved to righteousness. The former slavery, of which they were ashamed, produced death. The new slavery, however, produces righteousness with its resulting new life.

But there is also the question of occasional sin. Although believers are not in bondage to sin, is it all right for them to sin occasionally (v. 15)? The apostle answers, "God forbid." Believers who have had a changed leadership have no right to serve the old master. By sinning they would voluntarily put themselves under the old leadership. Now that they are free from the bondage of sin, they are to be servants to God. There is no excuse for believers to sin. God demands and expects holiness, and he has provided the way.

## POWERLESS SANCTIFICATION (7:1–25)

### 1. The Marriage of the Saint (7:1–6)

The apostle has carefully shown that there are two laws trying to operate in believers' lives. The first is the law of the sin nature, that from which believers have been delivered. The second is the law of grace, the principle of being united to Christ and living a life in accordance with divine principles.

The apostle uses the law of marriage to illustrate the problem of the sin nature in the lives of believers. The law for marriage is that a spouse is freed from his or her mate only by death (vv. 2–3). In the same way believers, who were once united to the sin nature, are now free from that sin nature because they have died to it. Moreover, believers are now united to Christ and are to serve him.

But now comes the problem. Although the believer has died to the sin nature, the sin nature is not dead. It is very much alive and wants the believer to serve it. The believer is therefore in the position of having two husbands: the old nature and the Lord Jesus Christ. Moreover, the first husband is always trying to get the believer back again.

But believers, who are separated from their old sin natures, are no longer obligated to serve them. In fact, if they serve their old natures, they are being unfaithful to Christ. They are therefore delivered from the law that once controlled them and should now be controlled by the Spirit of God.

### 2. The Purpose of the Law (7:7–14)

Before illustrating the frustration of believers who vacillate between two natures, the apostle turns to another important question. Since believers are free from the law and also free from sin, is it possible that the law and sin are in the same category? Is the law sinful?

The answer is "absolutely not." Knowledge of sin came by the law (v. 7). People sinned before the law was given, but they did not see the true character of their sin. The law *showed* what sin was, but it could not *solve* the problem. Only Christ could do that. But the law is holy (moral phase, shows us we are sinners), just (spiritual phase, shows Christ alone is the solution), and good (social phase, shows believers a new way of life) (v. 12).

## The Struggle of the Saint (7:15–25)

It would be impossible for believers to live the Christian life through their own power. They need the enablement of the Spirit of God. The apostle explains this provision in chapter 8. However, before explaining the available power, Paul deals with the utter helplessness of believers who try to live the Christian life by themselves. Believers must realize the futility of such an experience before seeing the necessity of the working of the Holy Spirit in their lives.

Believers who obligate themselves to their old sin natures are slaves to them (vv. 15–17). Believers cannot do what they want to do. Instead, they do those things they hate. The sin nature is not dead. And unless it is counteracted by the Spirit of God, it will control the believer.

Believers who find themselves in this situation are absolutely helpless (vv. 18–20). Although they try to war against their sin natures, it is self against self. The result is absolute failure.

As a result, believers are in constant turmoil and struggle. But who shall deliver the believer from this physical body that contains the sin nature? The answer is the Holy Spirit.

# 7

# *Abundant Christian Living*

*8:1–39*

> "We are more than conquerors
> through him that loved us"
> (Romans 8:37).

---

The eighth chapter of Romans is the high-water mark of this important book. As seen previously, believers are declared righteous by God because of faith in God's provision. But although believers are free from the penalty of sin, they are not necessarily free from the power of sin.

The old sin nature, which continues very much alive and active, constantly tries to manifest itself. The apostle emphasizes the complete frustration believers feel when he says, "For the good that I would, I do not: but the evil that I would not, I do" (Romans 7:19).

The Christian life is not merely difficult, but wholly impossible for those who try to live such a life all by themselves. But not only has God given us the standards he expects us to keep, he has also enabled us to keep them.

He has given every believer the Holy Spirit, who is the very person of God, not just a force or influence. God's answer to the problem of the Christian's sin is the empowerment of the Holy Spirit, and this great truth is set forth in this significant chapter. It is the positive answer to the problem presented in previous chapters.

The Holy Spirit is God's provision for abundant Christian living.

This chapter relates to chapters 1–7 of Romans as follows:

PART ONE: DOCTRINE (1–8)

The Doctrine of Sin (1:1–3:20)

The Doctrine of Justification (3:21–5:21)

The Doctrine of Sanctification (6:1–8:39)

- A. Positional Sanctification (6:1–10)
- B. Progressive Sanctification (6:11–23)
- C. Powerless Sanctification (7:1–25)
- D. Powerful Sanctification (8:1–39)
  - 1. The Power of Sanctification (8:1–17)
    - a. The deliverance from sin (8:1–9)
    - b. The end of the conflict (8:10–11)
    - c. The living of the life (8:12–17)
  - 2. The Products of Sanctification (8:18–27)
    - a. The hope of glory (8:18–25)
    - b. The help of the Spirit (8:26–27)
  - 3. The Praise of Sanctification (8:28–39)
    - a. The purpose of God (8:28–30)
    - b. The security of the believer (8:31–39)

## THE POWER OF SANCTIFICATION (8:1–17)

### 1. The Deliverance from Sin (8:1–9)

This chapter begins with the fact that there is no condemnation for believers. Although unbelievers will be judged for their sin, believers, who now have a perfect standing before God, will never stand in judgment for their sin. The judgment seat of Christ, in which believers partake, is a time of commendation, not condemnation (2 Corinthians 5:10). Believers have been forgiven all trespasses (Colossians 2:13), are not condemned (John 3:18), and are passed from death unto life (John 5:24). Their concern is not about sin's penalty, but about sin's power or dominion over them.

The starting point for the deliverance from the power of sin is their position "in Christ Jesus" (v. 1). They are delivered from sin's dominion because of where they are. Self-effort or the Mosaic Law does not deliver. Only Jesus Christ, the Deliverer, does. This is the basis for all Christian conduct. Believers are to become what they already are. They are to act in accordance with their perfect position.

Notice that the words "who walk not after the flesh, but after the Spirit" (KJV), are not in the *American Standard Version* and do not belong to the original text. Instead they go with verse 4 and concern the *enablement* for Christian living, not its basis. The believer's perfect position is in Jesus Christ and is obtained through faith in Christ's finished work at Calvary.

The reason for believers' deliverance from the power of sin is the new law that now operates in their lives (v. 2). The "law of sin and death" is the old sin nature, as explained in chapters 6 and 7. This law can still operate in believers' lives. However, they are set free from that law by allowing a new law, "the law of the Spirit of life," to operate in them.

How does this new law work? It operates by counteracting or superseding the old law. Believers still have their old natures, but now they also have the new law of the Holy Spirit. By relying on him, the law of the old nature is counteracted and the believer is freed from it.

This same principle operates every time an airplane flies. The law of gravity says it should never fly. But the law of aerodynamics counteracts that law and the airplane flies. The law of gravity is not eliminated but superseded.

Peter's experience (Matthew 14:22–33) is a good example of one law counteracting another. When he was walking on the water, the law of gravity said he should sink. But this natural law was superseded by another law and Peter walked on the water. The law of gravity was not changed but counteracted.

In the same way, reliance on the Holy Spirit does not eradicate the old sin nature but rather counteracts it. Although the old nature is still very much there, it is superseded by God's new law.

The old nature, however, has already been judged by God at the cross (v. 3). The purpose of this judgment was to fulfill the law of God, that is, his righteousness, in all who walk after the Spirit.

There are two walks we may follow: (1) the walk according to the flesh, the old sin nature, or (2) the walk according to the Spirit, the law of God, the law of righteousness. What products result from these two kinds of walks?

If we walk after the law of sin, sin results. If we walk after the Spirit, righteousness results (v. 5). The pattern of our lives depends on the law by which we are operating.

The natural consequence of living by the old nature is enmity against God (v. 7). Such people are out of harmony with God's purposes. They are living in disobedience to the Lord. Although they do not lose their salvation, they can produce only dead works. Believers living such lives are not able to please God (v. 8). Spiritual victory can never come from the old sin nature. It can never come from human effort. If we are to have freedom from the power of sin, it must come from God.

The Spirit of God has been given to the children of God to help them walk by the law of God (v. 9). Verse 9 should be rendered, "But you are not in the flesh, but in the Spirit, *since* the Spirit of God dwells in you." The Holy Spirit indwells all believers from the time they are converted to help them overcome the law of sin.

### 2. The End of the Conflict (8:10–11)

The question the apostle answers concerns when the conflict with the old sin nature will end and how to have victory over the old sin nature. The warfare between the two natures will continue until the resurrection of the body (v. 11). It is the resurrection of Christ that guarantees the resurrection of the believer.

In that yet future day of resurrection, the Holy Spirit will put the believer under an entirely new law, the law of life. If the Spirit of God is able to do such a thing then, he certainly can put believers under a new law now. This he does when believers permit him to do so.

### 3. The Living of the Life (8:12–17)

The apostle so far has presented the negative side of the Christian walk. Believers are delivered from sin and one day will be delivered from death. But there is also a positive side. Believers have a position as children of God, and their way of life should result from that fact.

Jesus Christ bears a relationship to the Father that no one else does. He is in essence God, so he is and always was related to the Father. Believers, however, become children of God because of the new birth, not because they have the essence of God. When we receive Christ as Savior, we are adopted as children of God.

This adoption has in view heirship. Believers are not equal heirs with Christ, however, but co-heirs or joint-heirs (v. 17). According to the Roman law at the time, if two brothers were equal heirs the property would be divided into two equal parts. However, if the same brothers were joint-heirs, both would have total rights to the total inheritance. The believer is a joint-heir with Christ. With Christ we possess the total inheritance of God.

## THE PRODUCTS OF SANCTIFICATION (8:18–27)

### 1. The Hope of Glory (8:18–25)

Believers, however, inherit not only the blessings of Christ but they share in the suffering of Christ caused by the hatred of the world. Deliverance from this will not come until the resurrection, but such suffering cannot be compared with the glory that will follow (v. 18).

All creation looks forward to the day when believers will be glorified, because then the curse upon creation will be lifted. When God created Adam, he gave him dominion over the earth. When Adam sinned, God cursed not only Adam but the earth over which he had dominion as well. One day the whole creation will have a rebirth. This is why it now "travails in pain," looking forward to that glorious day (v. 22).

Believers also suffer because they still have unredeemed bodies. They can be sure their bodies will be glorified, however, because God has given them the Holy Spirit who is the pledge that more is to come. Meanwhile, believers need patient hope while awaiting the fulfillment of the promise of God (v. 25).

### 2. The Help of the Spirit (8:26–27)

The apostle points out that groans emanate from creation awaiting redemption, from the believer awaiting a redeemed body, and from the Holy Spirit as he intercedes for believers. Although the redemption of both creation and the body of the believer will occur in the future, the help of the Holy Spirit in prayer occurs now.

The Holy Spirit reminds God of his purpose to bring believers to glory and thereby helps believers with their lack of patience and faith. The Holy Spirit's groanings are understood by the Father since the Spirit intercedes for believers, the special objects of divine favor, and since his groanings are always within the purpose of God.

## THE PRAISE OF SANCTIFICATION (8:28–39)

### 1. The Purpose of God (8:28–30)

The apostle has encouraged believers by showing them their future hope in glory and their present help from the Holy Spirit. But there is another reason for encouragement—the total purpose of God.

God does not work in a haphazard, unplanned manner. He is sovereignly moving all things for the welfare of those who are his own. Believers are the focal point for the future redemption of creation, a future redeemed body, and the present help of the Holy Spirit. And the entire program of God focuses on them. This is why all things work together for good to them that love God (v. 28).

The apostle uses several important words to describe the main aspects of God's overall program for believers. These words may be defined as follows.

a. Foreknew (Foreknowledge) (v. 29): The forethought of God in selecting believers for his purpose. It stems from God's omniscience and does not mean simply to know beforehand. Believers have been called into this relationship in accordance with God's eternal purpose.

b. Predestined (Predestination) (v. 29): The predetermination of the destiny of the saved and shows what God will do for them.

c. Called (Calling) (v. 30). The ability of God to draw people unto himself so they accept God's provision without ever being forced or coerced.

d. Justified (Justification) (v. 30): The act of God whereby he declares the sinner righteous on the basis of Christ's death and resurrection.

e. Glorified (Glorification) (v. 30): The future act of God whereby he delivers believers from every aspect of sin, including its very presence.

All of these verbs (vv. 29–30) are in the past tense and show that, as far as God is concerned, these facts are already completed. Because they are certain to occur, all things work together for the believer's good. Believers are the special objects of God's knowledge, and God has chosen those things to bring into their experiences that which will accomplish his ultimate purpose.

### 2. The Security of the Believer (8:31–39)

Since the entire program of God revolves around believers, God is for them. Then who can be against them? The same God who in holiness once condemned sinners now in righteousness defends believers. The same God who gave his only Son to redeem sinners now delights in giving believers all things (v. 32).

Verses 33, 34, and 35 begin with questions asking who could possibly be against believers so protected by God himself. Maybe there is someone who would want to make a charge against the elect of God (v. 33). But such a person is really making a charge against God. Since God is the Judge, he is the one who declared sinners righteous. To question such a decision is an affront to the Judge.

There may also be those who would like to act as judges and condemn believers (v. 34). But again, how can one condemn what God has already declared righteous?

Perhaps there is one who would snatch away believers by brute force (v. 35). Some of these natural enemies are tribulation, distress, persecution, famine—all areas of possible suffering for believers. But God has a purpose for each of them. They are stepping stones that reveal his glory through believers. Through such suffering, believers are more than conquerors.

As we examine the entire universe there is not one thing that can overthrow believers. Life or death—the sphere of existence cannot do it (v. 38). Angels, principalities, powers—the sphere of created beings cannot do it (v. 38). Things present, things to come—the sphere of time cannot do it (v. 38). Height or depth—the sphere of space cannot do it (v. 39). Since there is nothing before God or mankind that can separate believers from Christ, there is indeed no separation. What a privilege and peace to know that "if God be for us, who can be against us?" (v. 31). The chapter that opened with no condemnation closes with no separation. The believer is secure.

# 8

# Why God Chose Israel

*9:1–10:21*

> "For the Lord has chosen Jacob unto himself, and Israel for his peculiar treasure" (Psalm 135:4).

---

Frederick the Great, king of Prussia, had a court chaplain who tried at every opportunity to show him the truth of Scripture. Finally the king told the chaplain, "Show me just one reason why I should believe that the Bible is true." The court chaplain answered, "The Jews!"

The promise God made and kept concerning Israel shows the truth of Scripture. God has kept the covenant he made with Abraham that from him would come a great nation (Genesis 12:2). The existence of the nation of Israel shows the faithfulness of God.

The faithfulness of God is also at the heart of the book of Romans. Since it is God who has provided salvation for all mankind, this salvation depends on God's absolute fidelity. Can we conclude that God has always been faithful in his dealings with Israel?

From a casual observation of God's dealings with this nation, we might conclude that God is beginning a new work among people without completing what he promised Abraham, Isaac, and Jacob. After all, not all of God's covenants to this chosen nation have been fulfilled. Does it not appear that God's initial program for Israel has been set aside? If so, how can we be sure God will be faithful to us?

Chapters 9–11 discuss this issue and are therefore crucial to the entire book of Romans and to us. The apostle shows that although God has delayed his promises to Israel because of disobedience, he certainly has not cancelled them. Furthermore, his unrelenting faithfulness in dealing with that nation is an excellent illustration of the nature of his faithfulness to believers. God is faithful to Israel, God is faithful in providing salvation, and God is faithful in keeping and enabling those who accept his gracious provision. This section may be outlined as follows:

DOCTRINE (1–8)

DISPENSATION (9–11)

- A. Israel, Its Past (9)
  1. The Position of Israel (9:1–5)
  2. The Persons in Israel (9:6–13)
  3. The Selection of Israel (9:14–24)
  4. The Salvation of Gentiles (9:25–33)
- B. Israel, Its Present (10)

1. The Ignorance of the Way of Salvation (10:1–11)
2. The Ignorance of the Application of Salvation (10:12–13)
3. The Ignorance of the Proclamation of Salvation (10:14–21)

## ISRAEL, ITS PAST (9:1–33)

### 1. The Position of Israel (9:1–5)

Here Paul declares his love for his own Jewish people and his wish that they would accept God's salvation as he has. Their rejection of Christ, the Messiah, is a constant burden to him. In fact, this burden is so great that he is willing to be accursed if that would help them accept Christ (v. 3).

The problem with this nation, however, was not that she was ignorant of the message about the coming Messiah. It was that she had rejected the revelation God had given. Look, for instance, at the great place of privilege this nation enjoyed before the Lord. It is only of Israel that God said, "The LORD your God has chosen you to be a special people unto himself, above all people that are upon the face of the earth" (Deuteronomy 7:6).

The special position is described by the apostle (vv. 4–5). In a few short phrases Paul shows this nation all God gave them as the "special people unto himself." First was the adoption. Israel as a nation was adopted by God and made heir to the blessings of God (Exodus 4:22). Next was the glory. Israel as a nation was a channel of the glory of God (Exodus 13:21–22; 16:10). The covenants are also mentioned, a reference particularly to the four unconditional covenants God made with Israel: the Abrahamic (Genesis 12–15), the Palestinian (Deuteronomy 30), the Davidic (2 Samuel 7:12–16), and the New (Jeremiah

31:31–34). God promised that this nation would have a land, king, throne, and kingdom forever. Moreover, God would one day give the people a new heart and they would turn to him.

The apostle also mentions another covenant God made with Israel, the Mosaic Law. The purpose of the law was to give Israel a rule of life (Exodus 19:5–6; Deuteronomy 4:8).

Another privilege of this nation was the service of God, which included the holy days, priesthood, offerings, tabernacle, temple; in fact, all that looked forward to Christ (Hebrews 10:1–3). Israel also had the promises, the particular promises of the coming Messiah given throughout the Old Testament, beginning in Genesis 3:15. This nation also had the fathers—Abraham, Isaac, and Jacob—men who honored and feared God.

The climactic privilege of Israel, however, was that through this nation Christ would come according to the flesh (v. 5). No other nation could boast of such privilege or position. This nation had been singularly blessed by God, chosen by God, set apart by God, and highly privileged by God.

### 2. The Persons in Israel (9:6–13)

The problem with the nation Israel is not with the covenants but with those who received them. God's Word is true and God is faithful. But the people spurned their privileges and turned their backs on God.

At this point an important question arises. Wasn't it necessary for God to fulfill to all Israelites the covenants he made with this nation? And since these covenants are not now being fulfilled, how then is God faithful?

The apostle turns to the events of biblical history and shows that the human descendants of Abraham were not automatically the heirs of spiritual blessing. God's selection of his people was always by his mercy and grace, never by Israel's merit or self-effort.

The promises of God have always been for believers. For Jews to benefit, therefore, they must believe God. The apostle clearly states this principle: "For they are not *all* Israel, which are *of* Israel" (Romans 9:6).

The "all Israel" group refers to saved Israelites who make up only part of those who are natural Israelites. The apostle shows that Israelites were saved through individual belief, even though they had a unique position as part of the nation of Israel.

What examples may be used to prove this important point? The apostle presents two case histories, first Isaac and Ishmael (vv. 7–9) and then Esau and Jacob (vv. 10–13).

Although Isaac and Ishmael had different mothers, they had the same father. They were both natural sons of Abraham. But God said, "In Isaac shall your seed be called" (v. 7), showing the sovereign selection by God. In addition, Ishmael is called a child of the flesh, not of promise. This indicates his unregenerate state (v. 8).

Some might object to this illustration, however, for the mother of Isaac was more acceptable than the mother of Ishmael. So Paul gives another example, this one involving the twin sons of Isaac (Genesis 25:19–28).

It is a historical fact that Esau was older than Jacob and therefore, according to law, deserved his father's blessing. But God chose Jacob instead, not on the basis of human merit but by divine selection (v. 11). God's election therefore stems from God, not mankind.

### 3. The Selection of Israel (9:14–24)

If God's election comes from himself, there are two further questions that must be answered.

First a question from the divine side: "Is there unrighteousness with God?" (v. 14). In other words, is God completely fair or does he favor some?

The apostle answers with a Greek idiom, *me genoito*, which could be translated, "How awful that you could even think of such a thing!" There is absolutely no unrighteousness with God. He is completely fair. God is really being fair when he selects on the basis of his mercy and grace. God would be just in condemning all peoples of the earth if he chose to do so. The fact that he has selected any is because of his mercy and grace.

For instance, take the case of Moses (v. 15). Certainly he was not selected on the basis of merit or leadership. Moses even refused to be the leader when God asked him (Exodus 4). But God overruled in his life, and he was selected because of the mercy of God. If this was true with the leader of Israel, how much more so with those who followed? On the other hand, Pharaoh did not receive the grace of God. He hardened his own heart, and God amplified the judgment. The conclusion is that God has "mercy on whom he will have mercy, and whom he will he hardens" (v. 18).

Second, a question from the human side: Should we question the actions of God? (v. 19). Why is it, for instance, that God hardened Pharaoh's heart and then judged him? Is that really fair?

The apostle answers this question by showing that the very character of God is holy and righteous. God therefore cannot act unfairly. He must always act in holy and righteous ways. The real question is not, "Why did God not choose *all*?" but rather, "Why did God choose *any*?" Israel did not have a right to be chosen nor do any of us today. But the Potter has power over the clay (v. 21) and everyone he chooses is according to his mercy and grace, not because of natural selection or human merit. Creation does not have the right to challenge the Creator.

### 4. The Salvation of Gentiles (9:25–33)

Although the Jews had a special position before God, nowhere does Scripture state that they had a monopoly on salvation. All who believe are saved, whether they be Jews or Gentiles. Hosea 1:10 and 2:23 are quoted to show that the Lord would call those who were not his people (Gentiles), his people (vv. 25–26).

How, then, does this relate to Isaiah's prophecy that a remnant within Israel would be saved (v. 27)? The point is that a remnant would be saved, but Israel as a nation would reject the Messiah (v. 32). Gentiles, on the other hand, though never having had the privileges Israel enjoyed, did believe. Today, many Gentiles are still being saved.

## ISRAEL, ITS PRESENT (10:1–21)

### 1. The Ignorance of the Way of Salvation (10:1–11)

The apostle turns from God's gracious selection of Israel in the past to the present state of this people. The Jews, who thought righteousness came by heredity and conformity to the law, were ignorant of the way, application, and proclamation of salvation. The apostle explains these in this chapter.

Paul was the minister of the Gospel to the Gentiles but he did not rejoice in Israel's failure. His desire and prayer was that Israel would be saved (v. 1). What, then, was the problem with this nation? First, it had zeal, but not according to knowledge (v. 2). It was misguided. Moreover, it was a zeal *for* God, but not a zeal *from* God. It was misdirected.

Israel's main misconception was their belief that they could work to make themselves righteous rather than accept the righteousness God provides. They were trying to keep the Mosaic Law to gain God's approval. They were trying to establish their own righteousness so they would be acceptable to God on the basis of their own accomplishments. But people cannot save themselves. "There are none that do good, no, not one" (Romans 3:12).

The Mosaic Law was never intended to be God's final plan. It was given to show what sin is, to show the need of a Savior. Moreover, if righteousness could be obtained by keeping the law, only those who had the law could be righteous. How then could Gentiles be righteous? The fact is, righteousness does not come through the law, it comes through faith. Righteousness is possible for everyone because all have the opportunity to believe.

This seemingly new principle, that righteousness comes through faith, is not really new, however. As far back as the Palestinian covenant, the lawgiver Moses showed that the blessing of God comes by faith, not by works (v. 5; Deuteronomy 30). The Israelites missed the whole point. They thought righteousness came by keeping the law, but Moses said it came from the attitude of the heart. It comes by faith, not by works in any sense.

How, then, is this righteousness received? It comes simply by believing (vv. 9–10), which is why it is called "faith righteousness." It is received by faith and faith alone. The natural demonstration of this belief is the outward manifestation of the inner reality. For this reason, whoever believes will not be ashamed (v. 11).

### 2. The Ignorance of the Application of Salvation (10:12–13)

Although Jews had certain advantages before God, they did not have a special offer of salvation. The message of faith was given to Jews and Gentiles alike. If salvation is truly free, it must be universally available.

As far as God's salvation is concerned, there is no difference between Jew and Gentile. Both are sinners, both are under the penalty of sin, both need a Savior, and both are invited to accept God's provision. In other words, all who call on the name of the Lord will receive his gracious response. Since all are lost, all can be saved.

### 3. The Ignorance of the Proclamation of Salvation (10:14–21)

The problem concerning Israel does not lie in the Word of God but in Israel's disobedience to the Word.

Because God's salvation is for the world, it must be universally proclaimed. Israel had heard the message and should have passed it on to others. The apostle shows that there is no calling without faith, no faith without hearing, no hearing without preaching, and no preaching without sending (vv. 14–15).

The fact that faith comes by hearing and hearing by the Word of God (v. 17) shows that knowledge must precede faith. One must have the message to believe it. People can believe only what is presented to them. It is important therefore to make the message clear, to give unbelievers facts on which they can make a decision.

Although ignorance is the reason for Israel's condition, it is no excuse. Universal salvation requires a universal proclamation. God has given at least one such universal proclamation in the display of nature (v. 18). In addition, the Old Testament anticipates that God would send the message of salvation to every nation (vv. 19–21).

Even though Israel has rejected God's message, God is still waiting to receive Israel. He says, "All day long I have stretched forth my hands unto a disobedient and gainsaying people" (v. 21).

# 9

# *Israel's Glorious Future*

*11:1–36*

> "I will also cause you to dwell in the cities, and the wastes shall be builded" (Ezekiel 36:33).

---

The faithfulness of God is seen throughout the pages of Scripture, but perhaps nowhere more clearly than in God's dealings with the nation Israel. This nation was promised by God, chosen by God, prepared by God, and blessed by God. Yet in spite of all God gave Israel, the people deliberately sinned and turned their backs on him. In a time of deep apostasy Isaiah wrote, "Ah, sinful nation, a people laden with iniquity, a seed of evil-doers, children that are corrupters: they have forsaken the LORD, they have provoked the Holy One of Israel unto anger, they are gone away backward" (Isaiah 1:4).

But should the faithlessness of the nation cause God to deny his own faithfulness?

The apostle Paul answers this question by first examining Israel's divine election and her ignorance of God's dealings with sinners. The apostle shows what will happen to this nation in the future.

If God is long-suffering, merciful, and faithful in his dealings with Israel, he will certainly carry out his promises to believers today. And Israel does have a glorious future under the gracious hand of God. This section may be outlined as follows:

DOCTRINE (1–8)

DISPENSATION (9–11)

- A. Israel, Its Past (9)
- B. Israel, Its Present (10)
- C. Israel, Its Future (11)
  - 1. The Partial Rejection of Israel (11:1–10)
    - a. The Illustration of Paul (11:1)
    - b. The Intention of God (11:2a)
    - c. The Illustration of Elijah (11:2b–4)
    - d. The Institution of the Remnant (11:5–10)
  - 2. The Temporary Rejection of Israel (11:11–32)
    - a. The Result of Israel's Blindness (11:11–15)
    - b. The Illustration of Israel's Rejection (11:16–17)
    - c. The Admonition Because of Israel's Rejection (11:18–24)
    - d. The Promise of Israel's Restoration (11:25–27)
    - e. The Universal Way of Salvation (11:28–32)
  - 3. The Doxology (11:33–36)

## THE PARTIAL REJECTION OF ISRAEL (11:1–10)

### 1. The Illustration of Paul (11:1)

Although God is not dealing spiritually with the nation Israel at present, he will do so in the future. In this chapter the apostle asks and answers the question, "Has God cast away his people?" (v. 1).

The answer the apostle gives is "God forbid," the familiar Greek idiom that can be rendered, "Oh the horror of the thought that you could even consider such a thing!" God certainly has not cast off those he has chosen for himself, and the fact that he has chosen this people has already been stated in chapter 9.

But what examples show that God is still working with this nation, that God has continued to be faithful? One obvious example is the apostle Paul himself. The fact that Paul is an Israelite and is saved shows that God has not completely cast off his people (v. 1). The apostle was redeemed during this age and was a physical descendent of Abraham. If only one Jew were saved during this time, it would prove that God had not rejected Israel.

### 2. The Intention of God (11:2a)

Another reason we know God did not cast away his people is the sovereign relationship he has with them. His original purpose was that he would not cast them away, so how could he change his purpose? The very nature of the covenants he made with them—the Abrahamic, Palestinian, Davidic, and New—demanded that there be a future for Israel. And since God is unchangeable (Malachi 3:6), his present purpose must be the same as in the past. God disciplines his people on account of disobedience, but he cannot discontinue his promises to them. He is bound by himself.

God had a plan for the nation Israel from eternity past. He had an entire program for that nation and God cannot abandon such an overall and comprehensive plan in the middle of it. God will fulfill all he has promised.

### 3. The Illustration of Elijah (11:2b–4)

Another evidence that God had not cast away his people was Elijah's experience in a similar situation. Everything seemed to be going against him. Israel had spurned his message and turned their backs on God. There was great apostasy in the nation. It seemed that all the people had forsaken God's law. They had thrown down God's altars and killed his prophets. Elijah was the only one left, or so he thought, and on Mount Horeb he poured out his heart to God.

God's answer was one of encouragement and assurance. Elijah was not alone. God said, "Yet I have left seven thousand in Israel, all the knees that have not bowed unto Baal, and every mouth that has not kissed him" (1 Kings 19:18). Although Elijah thought all of the people had gone against the Lord, God assured him that 7,000 had not. God always preserves a remnant for himself.

### 4. The Institution of the Remnant (11:5–10)

Although apostasy was general in the days of Elijah and of Paul, it was not universal. Even though Elijah was unaware of the remnant of 7000, they were there. The apostasy, even at that time, was not total. There were still those who believed.

In the same way, there was a remnant of believers in the day of Paul (v. 5). The apostle and the other Jewish believers constituted a remnant according to the grace of God. The fact that there *was* a remnant shows that God, even then, was dealing with the nation according to his grace (v. 6). Israel as a nation had rejected God. If God had been dealing with them according to their works, his rejection would have been total. But since God acts according to his grace, he is at liberty to preserve a remnant. And since they were a righteous remnant we know they had obtained this righteousness because they had believed.

But what about others? What happened to those who had rejected the work of God? The apostle says they were "blinded" (v. 7), a word referring to their hardness of heart and meaning "to form a callus." Their constant rejection produced an irritation that built up a callousness, resulting in an inability to receive God's truth. The result was not a diminishing of God's revelation, but a spiritual insensitivity and blindness.

This blindness of Israel was predicted in the Old Testament (v. 8) when it said Israel would reject God's truth. Present events are the outworking of this prediction. However, Israel's blindness is only partial because God is saving those whom he will out of this nation today.

The others, because of their rejection, have become hardened and calloused to the light of God's revelation. They are blinded to the message of God.

## THE TEMPORARY REJECTION OF ISRAEL (11:11–32)

Not only has the blindness of Israel been partial in that many Jews are being saved in the present age, but her blindness is partial in that it is temporary. The result of

Israel's blindness and the ending of this blindness are the subjects of this section.

**1. The Result of Israel's Blindness (11:11–15)**

The apostle explains that Israel's unbelief resulted in stumbling but not in a total fall. The Jews were not *permanently* cut off from the blessings of the Old Testament covenants. God's rejection of Israel as a nation could not be permanent because God had given the Israelites the covenants, and the faithfulness of God to his Word demands the fulfillment of those covenants.

What was the result of all this? Through this situation God has brought Gentiles to salvation. He thus intended to provoke his people to jealousy and bring them back to himself (vv. 11–15).

**2. The Illustration of Israel's Rejection (11:16–17)**

The apostle gives a horticultural illustration to explain God's dealing with the nation Israel. God had chosen the nation for his own purposes and set her apart, which is evidently the meaning of the term *holy* in verse 16. His choice began with Abraham, the father of the nation, who is compared to the root of an olive tree. Since the root was holy, or set apart unto God, so also the tree and the branches were set apart. Many have concluded from this illustration that this olive tree is representative of the place of divine blessing in God's dealings. Israel enjoyed the privilege of that blessing even though the nation turned from Jehovah.

The apostle further uses this illustration to explain the nature of Israel's relationship to God. Because Israel has forfeited the position of divine blessing, some of the branches have been broken off the tree. Not all Israel has been removed, however, for Israel's rejection is only partial (see 11:1, 3–4, and 25). But the unbelieving element in the nation has been removed as the Old Testament predicted (11:8–10). Into the place of divine blessing a new group, believing Gentiles, has been grafted. The privilege of God's blessing now rests equally on that group who once were "aliens from the commonwealth of Israel, and strangers from the covenants of promise, having no hope, and without God in the world" (Ephesians 2:12). It is possible for Gentiles through salvation to be grafted into this place of divine privilege because the revelation of God is now directed to them. This has all come to pass because Israel rejected the message of God.

### 3. The Admonition Because of Israel's Rejection (11:18–24)

Anticipating a further problem, the apostle warns Gentile believers about boasting. Should those who now share this blessed position boast because of it? Paul continues the horticultural illustration by demonstrating that life is derived from the root. Life in the branches comes from being vitally linked with the tree; therefore, these believers should not boast in themselves. They have been grafted into the tree by faith and their attitude should be one of thanksgiving to God for what he has done. As God removed Israel from the place of blessing because of unbelief (v. 20), he is able to graft in Israel again, if they give up their persistent unbelief (v. 23). Branches that were originally part of a tree are easier to graft back into the stock of the tree.

**4. The Promise of Israel's Restoration (11:25–27)**

The grafting in again of believing Israel is not only possible, it is also predicted. The key verse is 25, which includes some important words. One of these words is *mystery*. The word here does not mean something mysterious or hard to understand. As used in Scripture, the word means that which was a secret until God chose to reveal it.

The secret God is revealing here is not that Gentiles would be saved, for there were Gentiles saved even during Old Testament times. The secret is rather that the blindness of Israel was both partial and temporary.

The word *blindness* is also an important word in this verse and was used previously in verse 7. The people of Israel had hardened their hearts and become blind because they had rejected the Messiah. But this blindness was partial, not total, and therefore Jews are being saved during this age. One of these is the apostle Paul (11:1).

But when will this partial blindness be lifted? Another important word is *until*. This blindness will last "*until* the fulness of the Gentiles is come in." This blindness will last until the full number of Gentiles is grafted into the olive tree, the place of divine privilege during this age.

The expression *the fulness of the Gentiles* is not the same as *the times of the Gentiles* (Luke 21:24). The times of the Gentiles refers to the time when Jerusalem will be trodden down with Gentiles, which will not be until the Second Coming of Christ. The fulness of the Gentiles, however, is the time when the Gentiles will be in the place of divine privilege, the place of prominence in the program of God. This will end at the rapture of the church, after which God will again deal with the nation of Israel.

After this blindness is removed "all Israel will be saved" (Romans 11:26). The expression "all Israel" refers to all regenerate Israelites. At this time Israel will be delivered from Gentile world domination.

Moreover, after the Deliverer comes to Zion (the Second Coming of Christ), he will also come out of Zion to judge the ungodliness in Israel. The ungodly will be cut off, and the remnant will enter the kingdom (compare Ezekiel 20:33–38).

### 5. The Universal Way of Salvation (11:28–32)

The mercy of God is evident throughout the summary of this section. Mercy is what God gives to the undeserving. If he gave it to those who deserve it, it would no longer be mercy. For this reason God was able to act toward Gentiles as he did. They were not originally in the place of divine blessing and in bringing them into it, God has showed his mercy to them.

God is also going to show his mercy to Israel. For him to do so, they must be in a place where they cannot say they deserve it. God has allowed Israel to come to a place of unbelief so he can show his mercy to them.

God has therefore concluded all in unbelief (v. 32), so he might have mercy on both Jews and Gentiles alike. He did not do this to judge them, but so he could have mercy on them.

## THE DOXOLOGY (11:33–36)

The truth of the sovereignty of God causes the apostle to break forth into a doxology expressing wonderment at the very character of God. This is also a fitting conclusion to this major division of the book. All of the mercy seen in these chapters is of him, through him, and to him; therefore the glory belongs to God alone (v. 36). The program of God for Israel shows that he is faithful. He will restore the nation as he promised.

# 10

# The Christian's Service

*12:1–13:14*

> "Let us wait on our ministering" (Romans 12:7).

---

The church at Rome needed to learn how to live and act. And the apostle Paul knew that for Christians to behave correctly, they must first believe correctly. There must be something for the mind to act on if there was to be anything for the heart to treasure.

Paul chided the nation Israel for having "a zeal of God, but not according to knowledge" (Romans 10:2). The only right foundation for right Christian duty is right Christian doctrine. The book of Romans was written to give this foundation so believers could build their practice on it.

God has saved believers from sin, justified them in his sight, and now they are to live in accordance with what God has done.

As zeal without knowledge is wrong, so also is knowledge without corresponding Christian conduct. Believers who have learned the great doctrines of Romans must carry them into their lives.

The apostle James admonished, "Be doers of the word, and not hearers only" (James 1:22).

In this climactic section of Romans, the apostle Paul admonishes believers to practice the principles of Christian living they have already been given. He shows how believers are to do this and suggests certain ways.

This section may be outlined as follows:

DOCTRINE (1–8)

DISPENSATION (9–11)

DUTY (12–16)

- A. The Duty in Service (12:1–13:14)
  - 1. The Service to God (12:1–2)
  - 2. The Service to Man (12:3–21)
    - a. The Relationship to Spiritual Gifts (12:3–8)
    - b. The Relationship to Believers (12:9–16)
    - c. The Relationship to Unbelievers (12:17–21)
  - 3. The Service to the State (13:1–7)
    - a. The Principle (13:1a)
    - b. The Reasons (13:1b–5)
    - c. The Responsibilities (13:6–7)
  - 4. The Service to Individuals (13:8–14)
    - a. The Principle Given (13:8–10)
    - b. The Motivation Enjoined (13:11–14)

## THE SERVICE TO GOD (12:1–2)

The basis of our service for God is our relationship to God. Those redeemed by God are to voluntarily present their lives to him. Everything they are and have belongs to the Lord, and they are to realize that in everything they do. The first two verses of this chapter are the basis for what follows.

The word *brethren* shows that what the apostle is asking can be done only by Christians. Some non-Christians imitate the Christian life. They try to live good, moral lives. They give to worthy projects. Some even use the language of Christians.

But the Christian life requires participation, not imitation. Only believers can live the life God demands. Anyone else is superficial and hypocritical.

The word *therefore* hinges all that has gone before to all that follows. These verses close the first eleven chapters, concluding the great mercies God provides the Christian. The believer's obligation results from the work God has done.

The word *present* pictures the priest of the Old Testament offering a sacrifice on the altar. Believers, already cleansed by the blood of Christ, are to present themselves as *living* offerings to the Lord.

The sacrificial life may not mean pain, hardship, and persecution. It is simply a life lived on behalf of another. This recognizes God's ownership. This once-for-all presentation has many lasting and continuing effects.

The word *body* means the righteousness given believers is manifested through the physical body. The body, once the instrument of sin (Romans 6:13), now is the instrument of God's righteousness.

The animals sacrificed during Old Testament times did not consent. By contrast, believers voluntarily sacrifice themselves to God, and that as living sacrifices, not dead ones.

The Christian life is not based on reason, but it is reasonable. Thus, in light of all that God has done for believers, the only response is to present their bodies to him. This is why it is our "reasonable service."

Moreover, there is no question that God accepts such sacrifice. This and only this is acceptable to him.

But there is also a negative side: that which believers are *not* to do. They are not to be conformed to this world (Romans 12:2). Believers, changed on the inside, cannot inwardly conform to this world. But they are not to conform outwardly either. Presented to the Lord for his purposes, they are not to be used for other purposes.

What pattern of life, then, are believers to follow? Their lives are to be *transfigured*, the word used of Christ on the Mount of Transfiguration when his inner reality shined forth in all its glory (Matthew 17:2).

Believers are changed within and they are to allow this inner reality to shine forth—first by salvation and then by the continual renewing of their minds by the Word of God. Believers must know what is correct before they can act correctly, and renewed action comes by a mind that is renewed by the Word of God.

The result of such a sacrificial life is that believers will prove [approve, discern, appreciate] the will of God. Their lives will conform to God's will and others will see that such a life is good, acceptable, and perfect. The Lord has provided everything for believers. And our first responsibility is to present our bodies to the Lord.

## THE SERVICE TO MAN (12:3–21)

### 1. The Relationship to Spiritual Gifts (12:3–8)

It is true that everything believers do affects their relationship to God. The apostle illustrates this relationship within the church, especially in regard to spiritual gifts.

When a person is saved, he or she becomes a member of the body of Christ. As the human body has many members—such as eyes, ears, hands, feet—so the mystical body of Christ has various members. These members are not only to exist, they are also to function.

The Holy Spirit gives each of these members at least one spiritual gift (Romans 12:6; compare also 1 Corinthians 12 and Ephesians 4). A spiritual gift is a God-given ability for service. Unlike Old Testament times when the Spirit of God came on certain people for special service, believers today are given an ability to minister for God at the moment of salvation.

Believers are also responsible to God to exercise their gift. For instance, a person with the spiritual gift of teaching the Word of God is to teach; a person with the gift of exhorting is to exhort; a person with the gift of administration is to administrate (Romans 12:7–8). Whatever our God-given ability, we are to exercise it for and unto the Lord.

The spiritual gifts of different believers complement and supplement one another, since not all believers have the same gifts nor does anyone have all the gifts. In the body of Christ the differing abilities of believers are necessary and important. No matter how small or seemingly insignificant a gift may appear, it is very important in the sight of God and in the ministry of the body. All believers therefore should know their gift or gifts, use them unto the Lord, and sense the unity and harmony of the body by encouraging others to exercise their gifts as well.

### 2. The Relationship to Believers (12:9–16)

Believers not only have a ministry within the fellowship of believers, they also have a relationship to believers. The apostle, in several succinct statements, instructs believers as to how they are to demonstrate their Christian lives before other believers.

First, love is to be without dissimulation (or hypocrisy). The word *dissimulation* was used of masked actors and means "without a mask." The love manifested by believers is to be genuine, without a mask. Only love shed abroad in hearts by the Holy Spirit can accomplish this (Romans 5:5).

Second, love is to be manifested by those who are brothers and sisters in Christ (Romans 12:10). Believers should seek every opportunity to manifest love. The word *business* (Romans 12:11) is better translated "zeal," meaning that believers are to be zealous, fervent, always seeking to put love into operation.

Hope lies in the future, tribulation is in the present, and prayer links both together (Romans 12:12). Love is to be manifested in meeting the needs of the saints and in pursuing opportunities for hospitality (Romans 12:13). Love should be extended to those who persecute believers and to those who rejoice and weep (Romans 12:14–15).

### 3. The Relationship to Unbelievers (12:17–21)

In regard to unbelievers, the apostle says believers are to be honest and to live in peace with them (Romans 12:17–18) and to leave vengeance to God (Romans 12:19). The

Lord is the judge of all, and he will express his wrath to those who do not trust him. Until then, believers are to bear witness of God's love. If believers render evil for evil, evil will be victorious. But when good is rendered for evil, evil is overcome (Romans 12:21).

## THE SERVICE TO THE STATE (13:1–7)

Here the apostle outlines for believers some spiritual obligations and responsibilities before the state. These are natural duties—those that arise because we are human beings, not because we are members of the church. We are citizens of a temporal state as well as of heaven.

### 1. The Principle (13:1a)

The relationship of believers to the state is to be one of subjection. This does not imply inferiority. The same idea is used of the relationship between husband and wife and between the Father and the Son (1 Peter 3:1; 1 Corinthians 11:3). This is a positional headship. Believers are subject to the state, not because the state is better but because the state has responsibilities believers do not have. This is a universal obligation—every soul is subject.

### 2. The Reasons (13:1b–5)

Believers are subject to the state because God has given civil authorities the responsibility for promoting that which is good. Whoever resists such authority also resists the ordinance of God.

What happens, however, if human government does not promote good and steps out of the area God has appointed for it? An illustration of such a situation is when the apostles were forbidden to preach and teach the Word of God in Jerusalem (Acts 5:17–29). Their answer was, "We ought to obey God rather than men" (Acts 5:29). In all else, however, believers are to be in subjection to government.

The purpose of the state is to preserve moral order (Romans 13:3). God, who is holy, wants to preserve righteousness and justice in his universe. When the state acts in harmony with God's will, it judges the wrong and approves the right. It bears the sword as the symbol of its God-given authority (Romans 13:4).

The submission of believers to the state is motivated by more than a fear of punishment. No power exists that is not ordained of God (John 19:11). This is not to say that God approves of every government, but he does sanction its existence. Therefore believers are to submit to the state because of their consciences (Romans 13:5). Their consciences will be grieved if they do not live peacefully under whatever government they find themselves. God has instructed believers to live peacefully with all people (Romans 12:18). Living peacefully with our neighbors and with our government promotes our Christian witness. Vengeance belongs to the Lord (Romans 12:19) and he will punish evil governments.

### 3. The Responsibilities (13:6–7)

How, then, are believers to show their subjection? What are their responsibilities? First, of course, they are to pay taxes. They pay these taxes in recognition of services received. When government renders services to its society, society must pay for them.

Believers are also to show honor and respect for those in governmental authority. This respect is due because of their position and power.

Furthermore, believers are also to pray for those in authority. We are told that "supplications, prayer, intercessions, and giving of thanks, [are to] be made for all men; for kings, and for all that are in authority" (1 Timothy 2:1–2). This special responsibility that believers have is a particular way they can honor governmental authorities.

## THE SERVICE TO INDIVIDUALS (13:8–14)

Believers bear a relationship not only to the state but also to individuals within the state who are looking for a genuine demonstration of the righteousness of God, a practical manifestation of the love believers preach.

### 1. The Principle Given (13:8–10)

The principle by which believers are to operate in relationship to others is the law of love. They are not to owe anything to anyone. Since other people judge believers by what they do and say, they are not to incur more debt than they can repay.

But there is a debt they are constantly to be repaying. It is the debt of love. They are "to love one another" (Romans 13:8). The word for love used here (*agape*) means that believers are to love while expecting nothing in return. In reality, only God can do that because humans love out of self-gratification, for what they personally can gain. But the love mentioned here is the love God produces in the believer's life, for "God is love" (1 John 4:8). Love is shed abroad in the believer's heart by the

Holy Spirit (Romans 5:5), and is the fruit of the Spirit (Galatians 5:22). This divine love is the possession of the child of God only.

Moreover, this love was the fulfillment of the Mosaic Law. By its nature the law was negative. It told people what they could not do. The law of love, on the other hand, in a positive way, shows why God's laws should be kept. Individuals will not injure their neighbors by committing adultery, killing, or stealing because they really love them (Romans 13:9). In every area of life Christians should conform to the law of love. Everything believers say and do must stem from this principle.

**2. The Motivation Enjoined (13:11–14)**

The great incentive for applying the principle of love is the Second Coming of Christ. Believers are to be always prepared for his return. They are to live in light of his coming.

The word *sleep* pictures apathy toward the believer's responsibilities, forgetfulness of God. Believers are to wake up and recognize the nearness of Christ's coming. They are to be prepared for battle.

Three times the apostle uses the phrase *let us* (Romans 13:12–13), showing the believer's obligations. First, believers are to cast off the works of darkness, as one taking off night clothes and dressing for the day. Next believers are to put on the armor of light and prepare for spiritual battle. Then they are to walk becomingly, to walk ready for Christ's return.

# 11

# Principles for Disputed Things

*14:1–15:13*

> "All things are lawful unto me,
> but all things are not
> expedient" (1 Corinthians 6:12).

---

The church at Rome was not perfect. Problems existed. The major need of its people was to know how to live the Christian life—how to apply what God had done for them. Before concluding his letter, the apostle deals with an important problem in the church at Rome and which has plagued believers throughout the centuries: the problem of the believer's relationship to other believers who hold to disputed things. The principles Paul gives are helpful not only for the church at Rome but for other believers as well.

This lesson is related to the previous one in that the law of love, expounded earlier, is applied to a particular situation. Believers who have been given the righteousness of God are to be living a life consistent with righteousness. Although they have responsibilities to the state and to the citizens or subjects of the state, they also have responsibilities to other believers.

The major obligation believers have to unbelievers is to lead them to Christ. The believers' responsibility to other believers is to preserve the unity and harmony of the body of Christ. The issues of peace and purity within the church are important ones, and the apostle gives principles as to how they may be preserved. This section may be outlined as follows:

DOCTRINE (1–8)

DISPENSATION (9–11)

DUTY (12–16)

A. The Duty in Service (12:1–13:14)

B. The Duty Concerning Disputed Issues (14:1–15:13)

1. The Problem Stated (14:1–2)
2. Principle No. 1: Liberty in Christ (14:3–12)
    a. Refrain from Judging Others (14:3–4)
    b. Recognize the Relationship to the Lord (14:5–9)
    c. Realize the Right of God to Judge (14:10–12)
3. Principle No. 2: No Cause of Stumbling (14:13–21)
    a. Refrain from Being a Cause of Stumbling (14:13)
    b. Recognize the Conscience of Others (14:14)
    c. Relinquish Rights on Behalf of Others (14:15–21)
4. Principle No. 3: God To Be Glorified (14:22–15:13)
    a. Glorify God by Not Condemning Others (14:22–23)
    b. Glorify God by Following Christ's Example (15:1–3)

c. Glorify God Through Unity (15:4–13)
  (1) Unity Through Hope (15:4)
  (2) Unity Through Glorifying God (15:5–6)
  (3) Unity Through Fellowship (15:7)
  (4) Unity Through the Body of Christ (15:8–13)

## THE PROBLEM STATED (14:1-2)

Within the church at Rome, as within churches today, there were those who gave undue attention to small, petty issues—their own peculiar scruples. The word *scruples* was originally the name of an extremely small Roman weight, and today we use the word *scrupulous* to refer to one who pays attention to unusual details, one who hesitates because of doubts or uneasiness, one who is unwilling to do something because of conscientious motives.

In the early church there were some who questioned everything and everybody, who set themselves up as self-appointed authorities on matters that had no bearing on what was right or wrong. They wanted all believers to conform to their ways of thinking, to abide by their scruples. Their attitude destroyed the peace and harmony of fellow believers, as did the attitude of the other believers in not accepting their scruples.

Until this point the apostle was speaking of the Christian life lived in full liberty by one believer with the other. But such was not possible in this situation because some were troubled about differences that had no moral significance. Scripture spoke plainly on those issues. But some thought that what others were doing was wrong, even though there was no moral significance in their action. These people were becoming authorities unto themselves, and all of this was dividing the church.

A certain issue brought this situation into focus. Some believers thought some days were more important than other days while other believers considered all days to be the same (Romans 14:5). Then, too, some thought they could eat only vegetables while others thought they could eat all things (Romans 14:2). The problem was compounded by Jewish Christians who had been taught the sanctity of certain days and diets. Gentiles also had questions as to whether or not they could eat meat that had been offered to pagan idols, which was more economical to buy than other meat (1 Corinthians 8).

These issues, which had nothing to do with moral matters, became important and began causing division. This confusion could have resulted in believers drifting away from the Lord, so their witness for Christ was at stake. What should be done about those who disagreed concerning disputed things?

The apostle deals with attitudes toward this problem, not the problem itself. After all, the issues involved were not important, but the attitudes they caused were. This is why both those who were weak (i.e., those who held to these issues) and those who were strong (i.e., those who did not) were admonished. The love they were to extend to unbelievers was now to be extended to other believers.

## PRINCIPLE NO. 1: LIBERTY IN CHRIST (14:3–12)

The apostle enumerates three important principles that regulate the conduct of believers as they face controversial areas that are neither right nor wrong as determined by the Word of God.

The first principle is that of liberty in Christ. Because of our position in Christ, believers have a liberty that we must regulate for ourselves. Once enslaved to sin, we are now enslaved to Christ.

Christian liberty does not mean license—that we are allowed to do anything we want to do. It means that we can do those things Christ wants us to do. The use of such liberty includes the following obligations.

### 1. Refrain from Judging Others (14:3–4)

All believers are to refrain from judging others. The apostle chides both the strong and the weak for their unloving nature (Romans 14:3).

The strong were not to laugh at the weak, and the weak were not to judge the strong. After all, both strong and weak were God's servants, not their own.

Believers who condemn other believers for decisions they make in cases where they are free to make them are taking the place of God. This is not to happen. God is able to discipline his servants, and he does so (Hebrews 12:5–11). Believers are therefore to refrain from judging other believers regarding controversial areas.

### 2. Recognize the Relationship to the Lord (14:5–9)

If we were to analyze the underlying motives of both points of view, we would find that both actions stem from the same incentive: to serve the Lord. This is the starting point for both.

Therefore, the important point is that people on both sides of an issue be fully persuaded that they are serving the Lord (Romans 14:5). If they are, they should not be subject to examination by fellow believers.

For instance, those who regard one day above another must be persuaded in their own minds that they are serving the Lord by doing so. Those who eat only vegetables must believe they are doing so unto the Lord. Those who do not regard such days or diets must also believe that what they are doing is unto the Lord. The apostle is not dealing with the results of these issues, but rather with the motives and the attitudes they cause.

The basis on which this operates is that both those who have certain scruples and those who do not are related to the Lord.

Whether believers live or die, in fact, all that they do is to be unto the Lord (Romans 14:8). Believers are God's servants totally. The question is this: Are you fully persuaded that you are serving the Lord by the position you take on a particular issue?

### 3. Realize the Right of God to Judge (14:10–12)

If believers are not to judge others, who will remedy an unjust situation? Since it is Christ who is Lord of all, he alone is qualified to judge all. This means that he will judge both the strong and the weak. The weak believer has no right to judge the strong, and the strong has no right to despise the weak. It is God who will take care of both.

The attitudes of both the weak and strong are wrong and both will stand before the judgment seat of Christ, where God will judge not only actions but also motives (2 Corinthians 5:10). Believers are therefore responsible to the Lord, and it is he who will judge the believer's stewardship.

## PRINCIPLE NO. 2: NO CAUSE OF STUMBLING (14:13–21)

It was Cain who first asked of the Lord, "Am I my brother's keeper?" (Genesis 4:9). Paul would reply, "Yes, you are." The believer *is* the keeper of his brother in the area of controversial issues. Here the apostle gives another principle: believers are to give no cause for stumbling. Believers are to curtail their own liberty for the good of other believers.

### 1. Refrain from Being a Cause of Stumbling (14:13)

The phrase *stumbling block* refers to an action of the believer whereby another is shocked and may be led into sin. Believers are not to judge other believers. Instead, they are to judge themselves, to determine carefully their own course of conduct, refraining from anything that might cause stumbling.

### 2. Recognize the Conscience of Others (14:14)

Here the apostle begins claiming the added authority of the Lord Jesus. The point he makes is that nothing he is discussing is unclean of itself. These issues are disputed matters, but they are not unclean or sinful.

Even though the issue in and of itself may not be sinful, the fact that it bothers the conscience of one believer may make it sinful for another believer. All believers must respect the feelings and attitudes of others, even though they may be indifferent to the issue themselves.

### 3. Relinquish Rights on Behalf of Others (14:15–21)

Although one believer may not share the scruples of another believer, he or she must nevertheless respect them. The believers to whom the issue seems unimportant are to relinquish their own rights for the love of their Christian brother or sister.

After all, if Christ has died for this person, cannot believers at least give up some favorite food for his or her spiritual well-being? It is true that all believers are free, but that freedom is limited by love for other believers. After all, the kingdom of God is not made for eating and drinking anyway. It is to show forth righteousness, peace, and joy in the Holy Spirit, and this is to other believers as well as to unbelievers (Romans 14:17).

Those who follow these principles are doubly rewarded (Romans 14:18). They are serving Christ through their motives and actions, which are acceptable to God. And they are approved of others.

The Christian life is not one of mere negativism; it contains positive injunctions as well. Both the strong and the weak are to follow after those things that produce peace and edification (Romans 14:19). The things involved with peace produce harmony and fellowship. The things that produce edification instruct believers in their privileges and position.

As a summary of this section, the apostle warns believers that they should do nothing to cause others to stumble or to make them weak (Romans 14:21).

Should believers not relinquish their rights, then the weaker person might be repelled (Romans 14:15), the strong person's testimony may be disrupted (Romans 14:16), the peace of believers may be disrupted (Romans 14:19), and the weak person may be led into sin (Romans 14:21). How important to relinquish one's own rights when so much is at stake!

## PRINCIPLE NO. 3: GOD TO BE GLORIFIED (14:22–15:13)

Everything believers are and do should bring glory to the Lord. This is the apostle's third principle, and he deals with it last.

### 1. Glorify God by Not Condemning Others (14:22–23)

The strong are to be commended for their faith. But such faith is to be toward God, not paraded before others. If the strong are right in their liberty, this is a matter with the Lord and it should bring glory to him.

But the weak are also cautioned. If they have any doubt about what they are doing, if they are not fully persuaded that it is right, they should not do it. If they cannot exercise faith about it, the action is wrong. Their attitude before God is important, and this attitude will be shown in their relationship to others.

### 2. Glorify God by Following Christ's Example (15:1–3)

The word *bear* in Romans 15:1 is the same word used of Jesus bearing his cross (John 19:17). It does not mean to tolerate the weak person but to give assistance. The weak person is not necessarily right, but is to be assisted by the strong person.

It is right to please others; to live for self is forbidden (Romans 15:1). Believers are to give up liberty on behalf of others.

The supreme example of giving up liberty on behalf of another is Christ's coming to die for the sins of the world. He was the one who "made himself of no reputation, and took on himself the form of a servant, and . . . became obedient unto death, even the death of the cross"

(Philippians 2:7–8). He gave up his rights and privileges, his own liberty, to become the sin-bearer of mankind. In light of this should not the strong give up their liberty on behalf of those who are weak?

### 3. Glorify God Through Unity (15:4–13)

#### *a. Unity Through Hope (15:4)*

Another reason believers are to give up liberty for the cause of others is their confidence in God's future, their hope. The trust of believers should be in Christ, and such petty disputes should strengthen that hope, not dim it. After all, tribulation "works patience; and patience, experience; and experience, hope" (Romans 5:3–4). For this reason, believers are to rejoice in hope and glory in tribulation. Such a hope unites believers rather than dividing them.

#### *b. Unity Through Glorifying God (15:5–6)*

Believers should also be willing to give up liberty since they are to live according to the character of God. The Lord is the God of patience and consolation. When the believers live in harmony with others, they are demonstrating the character of God, bringing glory to him.

#### *c. Unity Through Fellowship (15:7)*

Believers should be willing to give up their own individual liberty and receive each other, since God has received both the strong and the weak. The petty differences of the Roman believers were not of the Lord. Christ had received both groups for his glory, therefore they should receive one another.

### *d. Unity Through the Body of Christ (15:8–13)*

Believers should also be willing to give up their individual liberty for the sake of the body of Christ. Both Jew and Gentile were redeemed by God for his own glory. If both of these divergent groups were united for the glory of God, could not these with much lesser disputed matters also live in fellowship? The unity of the body of Christ is therefore an object lesson to all who have any problem of disharmony. The apostle's prayer is that the God of hope may fill each one, both strong and weak, with joy and peace. There is to be peace among believers, and the Lord can produce it if believers will simply let him.

# 12

# Paul's Personal Testimony

*15:14–16:27*

> "Paul, a servant of Jesus Christ" (Romans 1:1).

---

Romans is a book of instruction and of exhortation. By way of instruction, it lays the doctrinal foundation for the Christian life and witness. By way of exhortation, it admonishes believers to live in accordance with the spiritual riches they possess. Believers have responsibilities in every area of life: before God, in the church, under the state, to other believers. Some of these obligations have been pointed out by the apostle Paul in his epistle to the Romans. Other epistles emphasize other duties, all of which are applied by the Spirit of God. The Christian life is a triumphant life when lived according to God's instruction.

The apostle Paul himself is an example of such a life. Elsewhere he said, "Be followers [imitators] of me, even as I also am of Christ" (1 Corinthians 11:1). His point is that as he was following Christ in the areas about which he wrote, so believers were to follow him. A spiritual leader's example should be followed, and must be worthy to be followed.

The word *epistle* means "letter," and the epistle to the Romans is a letter from the heart of the apostle and the mind of God. In this last section, Paul tells some of the reasons for writing this letter and extends greetings to those he knew. It is a personal testimony of God's righteousness in his own life. This section may be outlined as follows:

DOCTRINE (1–8)
DISPENSATION (9–11)
DUTY (12–16)
- A. The Duty in Service (12:1–13:14)
- B. The Duty Concerning Issues (14:1–15:13)
- C. The Duty of Paul (15:14–16:27)
  1. The Purpose of Paul (15:14–21)
     - a. His Commendation of Them (15:14)
     - b. His Compassion for Them (15:15–21
  2. The Plans of Paul (15:22–33)
     - a. His Desire to See Them (15:22–29)
     - b. His Desire for Their Prayers (15:30–33)
  3. The Praise of Paul (16:1–27)
     - a. His Commendation (16:1–2)
     - b. His Greetings (16:3–16)
     - c. His Warning (16:17–20)

d. His Greeting From Others (16:21–23)
e. His Benediction (16:24–27)

## THE PURPOSE OF PAUL (15:14–21)

### 1. His Commendation of Them (15:14)

The apostle begins by striking a warm note of affection for the believers at Rome. He had spoken very strongly to them regarding matters of personal conduct. But he had done this to encourage them in their Christian lives, not to condemn them. He was aware of their spiritual earnestness, and now he tells them so.

The apostle not only commends their spiritual uprightness but also their ability to impart spiritual knowledge to others. With such increased knowledge comes added responsibility.

### 2. His Compassion for Them (15:15–21)

The apostle wrote to instruct these people concerning their Christian conduct, and in so doing he also fulfilled God's purpose for himself. He had been appointed to be an apostle by the Lord and was fulfilling his obligation to the one who had called him.

The picture is one of a priest offering sacrifices to God (Romans 15:16). The word *minister* means a "priestly minister," the word *ministering* means "sacrificing," and it was the Gentiles who were offered to the Lord. As the Old Testament priest offered sacrifices to the Lord, so Paul offered his life of service. His was a priestly ministry, and the Gentiles he won to Christ were a thank offering to God.

Some may consider such a life of service one of personal glory. But not so Paul. His was a life through which the

Lord was working, and therefore Christ should receive the glory (Romans 15:18). Paul preached and worked by the power of God, and both word and deed were accomplished by the Lord.

The apostle's message was authenticated by signs and wonders and the power of the Holy Spirit. This was not unusual, for Paul was an apostle, and God used the gift of apostleship to establish the church (Ephesians 2:20). As the prophets of old had their messages authenticated, so God authenticated the messages used to establish the church. Today we have the completed Word of God and such sign gifts are no longer necessary.

How far had Paul traveled to preach the Gospel of Christ? In a day when travel was by wind on the sea and by shoe leather on land, it could not have been far. Yet Paul writes that he had preached all the way from Jerusalem to Illyricum (Romans 15:19). The city of Jerusalem formed the eastern boundary of Paul's missionary travels. Early in his ministry he had preached in Jerusalem, and he was yet to revisit the city. The western most region Paul visited was Illyricum, which was located northwest of Greece along the Adriatic Sea. Perhaps he had viewed this area on his way to Thessalonica. The distance between these two boundaries was almost twelve hundred miles, and he had covered certain territories in this area many times.

Paul had fully preached the Gospel according to his gift of apostleship. Since an apostle was one who laid the foundation for the church, Paul had sought to preach the Gospel in places where Christ had not been named. It is evident from the instruction given in the book of Romans that Paul also had the gift of pastor-teacher (Ephesians 4:11). But Paul sought to use the best gift, the first one in order of priority that God had given him. He therefore took the message to those who had never heard it. This principle was also illustrated by the prophet Isaiah (Isaiah 52:15; Romans 15:21).

## THE PLANS OF PAUL (15:22–33)

### 1. His Desire to See Them (15:22–29)

Paul had not yet visited the people in Rome because of the pressing necessity to preach in other areas. He had been prevented from going to them earlier because he needed to complete his other ministry first. He had the responsibility to stay in one place until the work there was finished.

He had had opportunities to go to Rome, especially when he was at Corinth. Many ships made regular runs from Corinth to Rome. But instead of going at that time, he stayed to complete the work God had given him to do. The Lord has a particular time for every one of his purposes.

Paul's other obligations, however, did not diminish his love for the Roman believers nor his desire to visit them (Romans 15:23). Since the founding of the churches in the other areas had been completed, he would soon be able to make his journey to them.

The city of Rome, however, was not the apostle's ultimate destination. Since he had almost completed his God-given ministry in the east, he thought he soon could begin in the west. He was therefore planning to go to Spain and would make a stopover in Rome to see these believers (Romans 15:24). Little did he know what was ahead.

At that time in history, Spain formed the limits of the Gentile world. Since Paul was the minister of God to the Gentiles, he believed the remainder of his work would be there. Rome, however, would be on his way, and he would stop to see these believers.

Paul still had one more obligation, one more duty to perform before he could depart for Spain. He had to go to Jerusalem to deliver the gifts given to the church there by the churches of Macedonia and Achaia, modern-day Greece (Romans 15:25–27).

The wealthy class in Jerusalem was a vehement opponent of the Christian faith. As a consequence, the church in Jerusalem, though spiritually rich, was financially very poor.

And so it was that the churches in Macedonia and Achaia took up offerings for the church at Jerusalem. The churches throughout Greece had gained much spiritually from the church at Jerusalem, and so it was their duty to minister to them by giving of their material substance.

Paul had ministered to both churches, so he felt it was his duty to take the gift to Jerusalem. He wanted to make sure every penny of the money was delivered so the Jerusalem church would know they had spiritual fruit through him in the churches of Greece (Romans 15:28). After this, he planned to go to Rome, taking the blessing of the Gospel to them (Romans 15:29).

### 2. His Desire for Their Prayers (15:30–33)

The apostle appeals to believers at Rome to pray for him while they wait for him. Although he was absent from them, they were co-laborers with him and could pray for him. He appealed to them for prayer for the sake of the

Lord Jesus Christ and for the love of the Spirit (Romans 15:30).

Paul gives these believers specific prayer requests. They were to pray that he might have physical deliverance from the unbelieving Jews in Jerusalem. Even within the church, many Jews were not willing to welcome Gentiles into the body of Christ. In addition, the Romans were also to pray that the gift he was taking to the church at Jerusalem would be received. The gift was from basically Gentile churches to a Jewish church, so Paul prayed that a racial issue would not be raised and that the gift he carried would be gladly accepted.

The purpose of his prayer was that he would have joy in coming to them (Romans 15:32). Even coming to them in chains, as he did, could not destroy this joy. God's will is always best, even in such a situation for such an apostle.

## THE PRAISE OF PAUL (16:1–27)

Although Paul had not visited Rome when he wrote the epistle of Romans, he had many friends there. This final chapter of Romans shows his intense interest in and love for people. Thirty-five names are listed in this chapter, most of them mentioned only here. All of them, however, illustrate the practical personal righteousness and love of which the apostle previously wrote.

### 1. His Commendation (16:1–2)

Phoebe is commended first to the church at Rome. She was evidently the one who carried this epistle to these people. She was traveling from Cenchreae, the seaport of

Corinth, to Rome on business and provided the opportunity for Paul to send his letter to the believers there.

She is commended to the church because she is a sister in Christ and because she has been a servant in the church, ministering to the sick, poor, and needy.

**2. His Greetings (16:3–16)**

In this section Paul sends greetings to fifteen individuals, most of them unknown to us. Priscilla and Aquila, however, are known, having been companions of Paul (Acts 18:2, 18, 26). They had been driven from Rome, and now, having returned, had a church in their home.

Epaenetus, judging from his name, was a Greek and was a first-fruit of the Gentiles in Asia. Nothing is known of Mary (Romans 16:6); Andronicus and Junias are addressed as kinsmen, meaning his fellow-countrymen (Romans 16:7).

Especially interesting are Tryphaena and Tryphosa (Romans 16:12), whose names mean "delicate" and "dainty." These two sisters instead of being known for their delicacy, however, were known for their labor in the Lord. Rufus (Romans 16:13) may have been the son of Simon, the one who helped carry Christ's cross (Mark 15:21). The others are unknown.

**3. His Warning (16:17–20)**

The apostle next warns of the potential danger at Rome that could destroy the harmony and unity they enjoyed. Throughout Paul's ministry there had been many opponents to the Gospel, especially the Judaizers who disrupted the work of God almost everywhere Paul went. He knew they would eventually get to Rome.

The apostle gives an admonition to avoid fellowship with those who would cause such divisions. These opponents of Christ are characterized by deceitfulness, serving their own ends and purposes rather than the Lord's. Since God is the God of peace, they could not be of the Lord, and God would bruise them, who were evidently workers of Satan (Romans 16:20).

**4. His Greetings From Others (16:21–23)**

The apostle had sent greetings to many at Rome, and now those laboring with Paul sent greetings as well. Timothy is well known, and Lucius, Jason, and Sosipater are mentioned elsewhere (Acts 13:1; 17:5; 20:4). Tertius (Romans 16:22) acted as Paul's secretary in recording this epistle and also sent his greeting.

Gaius (Romans 16:23) was one of the first converts at Corinth (1 Corinthians 1:14) and Paul's host. Erastus was the treasurer of the city, showing that people of position had accepted the Gospel message. Quartus means "four." He had evidently been a slave, for many slaves had only numbers as names. The Gospel changes the lives of all, those of high position and those of low position.

**5. His Benediction (16:24–27)**

The apostle began this book with the prayer that he might "impart unto you some spiritual gift, so you may be established" (Romans 1:11). That prayer is now answered, for through these pages he indeed has imparted such a gift.

The Gospel Paul preached, the preaching of Jesus Christ, established believers. The mystery (Romans 16:25) was the divine secret that Gentiles would be fellow-heirs with Jews in the body of Christ (Ephesians 3). The Gospel brought Gentiles to glory and so glory came to God. Only the Lord could have such a plan as this, and all believers are the benefactors of it. "To God only wise, be glory through Jesus Christ forever. Amen" (Romans 16:27).

The triumphant Christian life is not a worthy option. It is the result of the believer's unity with Christ and is empowered by the Holy Spirit. Believers therefore are to live a life of spiritual action, one in which they apply the provision God has made. This is why they are to put on, as a garment, the Lord Jesus Christ, to live what they already are. Moreover, they are not to make provision for the flesh (Romans 13:14). If believers are dead to the old sin nature (Romans 6:2), they should not feed it. All their thoughts and attitudes should be directed by the Christ they serve.